AGES OF HAWAI'I

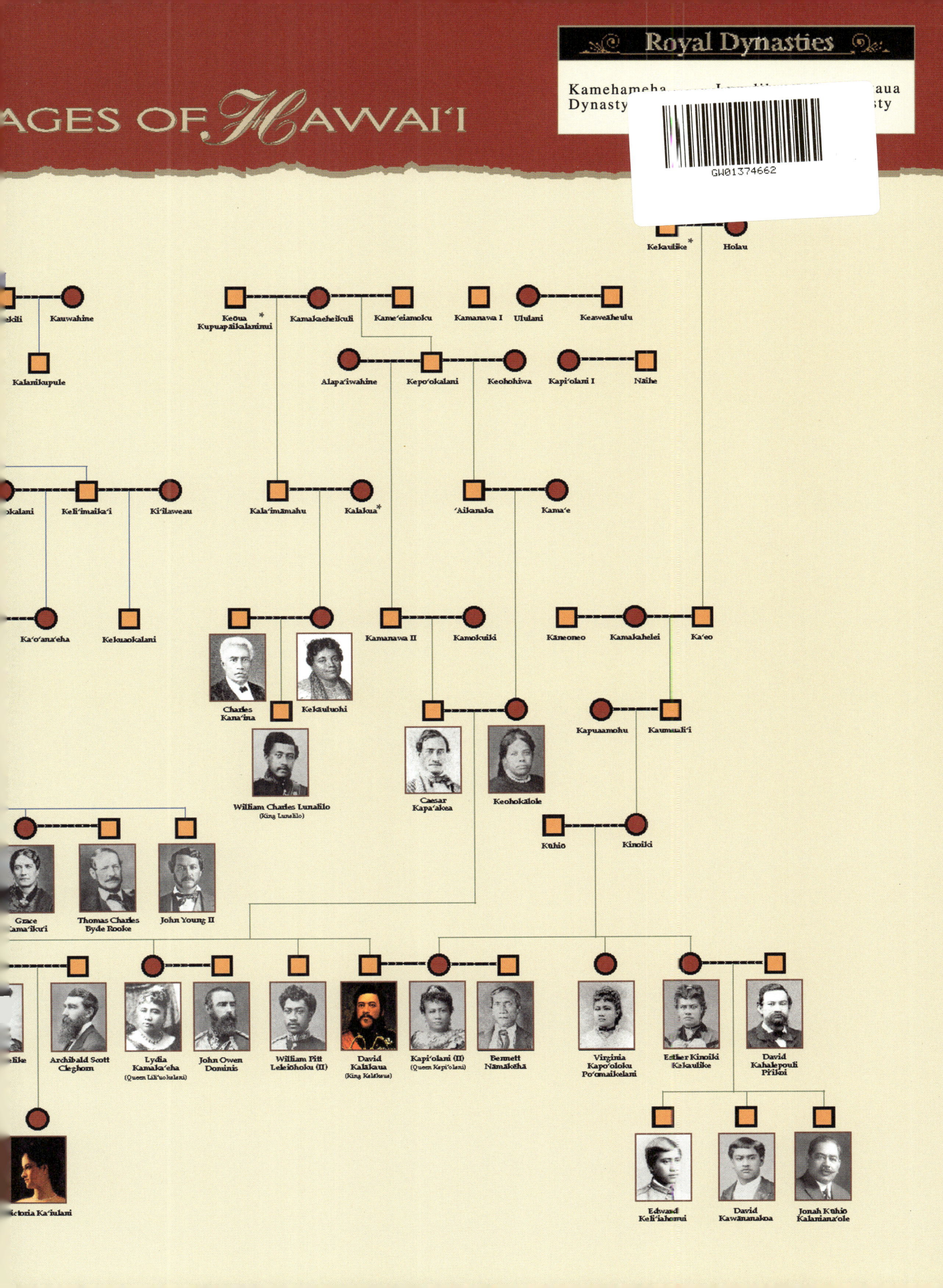

Royal Dynasties

Kamehameha Dynasty · Lunalilo · Kalākaua Dynasty

Genealogy Chart

- Kekaulike* — Holau
- ...kili — Kauwahine
- Keōua Kupuapāikalaninui* — Kamakaeheikuli — Kameʻeiamoku — Kamanawa I — Ululani — Keaweaʻheulu
- Kalanikupule
- Alapaʻiwahine — Kepoʻokalani — Keohohiwa — Kapiʻolani I — Naihe
- ...okalani — Keliʻimaikaʻi — Kiʻilaweau
- Kalaʻimamahu — Kalākua* — ʻAikanaka — Kamaʻe
- Kaʻōanaʻeha — Kekuaokalani
- Kamanawa II — Kamokuiki — Kameonео — Kamakahelei — Kaʻeo
- Charles Kanaʻina — Kekāuluohi
- Kapuaamohu — Kaumualiʻi
- William Charles Lunalilo (King Lunalilo)
- Caesar Kapaʻakea — Keohokālole
- Kuhio — Kinoiki
- Grace Kamaʻikuʻi — Thomas Charles Byde Rooke — John Young II
- ...like — Archibald Scott Cleghorn — Lydia Kamakaʻeha (Queen Liliʻuokalani) — John Owen Dominis — William Pitt Leleiōhoku (II) — David Kalākaua (King Kalākaua) — Kapiʻolani (II) (Queen Kapiʻolani) — Bennett Nāmākēhā — Virginia Kapoʻoloku Poʻomaikelani — Esther Kinoiki Kekaulike — David Kahalepouli Piʻikoi
- Victoria Kaʻiulani
- Edward Keliʻiahonui — David Kawānanakoa — Jonah Kūhiō Kalanianaʻole

THE HAWAIIAN MONARCHY

Dedicated to the memory of the late H.J. Bartels, 1945–2003,

curator, historian, scholar, admirer, aficionado of Hawai'i's ali'i.

THE HAWAIIAN MONARCHY

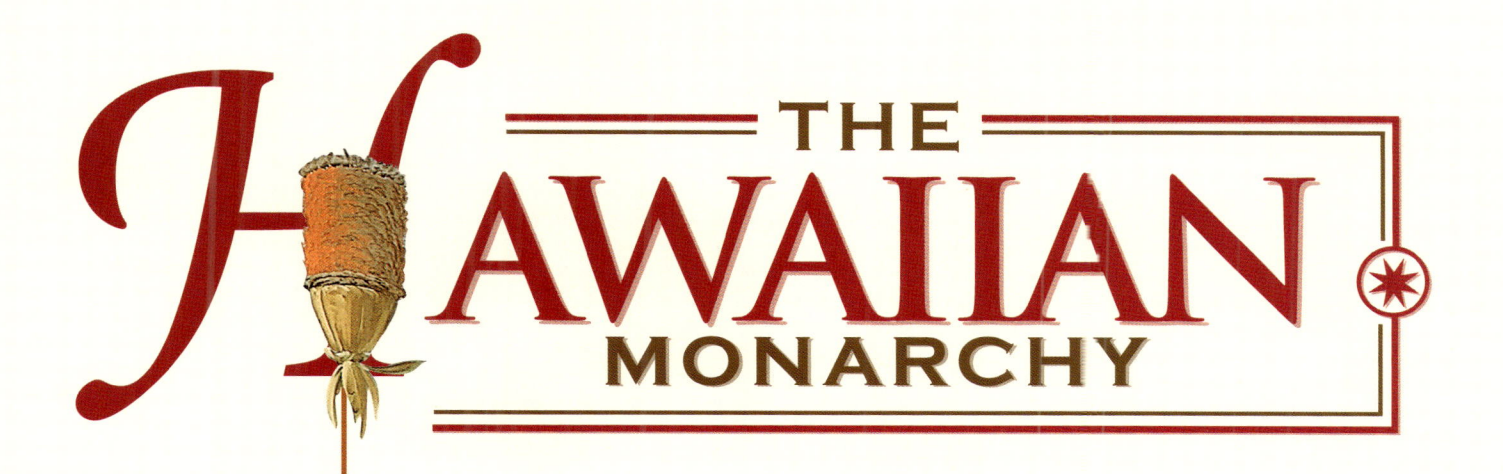

by Allan Seiden
with images from the Hawaiian Legacy Archive

MUTUAL PUBLISHING

1
2
Kamehameha IV
3
7
Queen Emma
8
Princess Likelike
9
15
10
14
19
20

Prince Leleiohoku

Kaahumanu

Queen Liliuokalani

Prince David

Princess Ruth

Previous Page: This composite photograph honoring the Hawaiian monarchy includes members of the Kamehameha and Kalākaua dynasties and King Lunalilo, as well as their consorts and important sites:

1. King Lunalilo
2. King Kamehameha IV
3. King Kalākaua
4. Queen Kapiʻolani
5. Prince Leleiōhoku
6. Queen Kaʻahumanu
7. Queen Emma
8. Princess Likelike
9. Princess Kaʻiulani
10. Statue of King Kamehameha I
11. Queen Liliʻuokalani
12. Kamehameha III
13. Prince David Kawānanakoa
14. Aliʻiolani Hale, or Government Building
15. Prince Jonah Kūhiō Kalanianaʻole
16. ʻIolani Palace
17. Princess Bernice Pauahi Bishop
18. Princess Ruth Keʻelikōlani
19. Hawaiian Coat of Arms
20. Kamehameha II
21. Honolulu Harbor
22. Kamehameha V
23. Royal Mausoleum at Mauna ʻAla.

Originally published in 1992 by Mutual Publishing
as *Hawaiʻi The Royal Legacy.*

This revised edition copyright © 2004 by Mutual Publishing

No part of this book may be reproduced in any form or
by any electronic or mechanical means, including information
storage and retrieval devices or systems, without prior
written permission from the publisher, except that brief
passages may be quoted for reviews.

All rights reserved
ISBN 1-56647-648-8
Library of Congress Catalog Card Number: 2004103025

First Printing, October 2005
1 2 3 4 5 6 7 8 9

Design by Sistenda Yim

Mutual Publishing, LLC
1215 Center street, Suite 210
Honolulu, Hawaiʻi 96816
Phone: 808-732-1709
Fax: 808-734-4094
Email: mutual@mutualpublishing.com
www.mutualpublishing.com

Printed in Korea

TABLE OF CONTENTS

Glossary	ix
History Makers of the Hawaiian Kingdom	xi
Rulers of the Kingdom of Hawai'i	1
Chapter 1: A MILLENNIUM OF ISOLATION	2
Chapter 2: ROYAL REGALIA	6
Chapter 3: KAMEHAMEHA	13
Chapter 4: LIHOLIHO/KAMEHAMEHA II	19
Chapter 5: KAUIKEAOULI/KAMEHAMEHA III	23
Chapter 6: ALEXANDER LIHOLIHO/KAMEHAMEHA IV	29
Chapter 7: LOT KAMEHAMEHA/KAMEHAMEHA V	35
Chapter 8: WILLIAM CHARLES LUNALILO	41
Chapter 9: THE ROYAL WOMEN	45
Chapter 10: DAVID KALĀKAUA	57
Chapter 11: ROYAL RESIDENCES	73
Chapter 12: LYDIA KAMAKA'EHA/LILI'UOKALANI	85
Chapter 13: VICTORIA KA'IULANI	101
Chapter 14: THE ALI'I LEGACY	109
Chapter 15: THE TWENTY-FIRST CENTURY AND BEYOND	113
Chronology of Important Events	122
Bibliography	129
Photo Credits	131
Index	133

Nā Leo Hano

(Listening to Many Voices, We Seek the Truth)

"According to the Hawaiian account, the Hawaiian islands were born when Papahānaumoku, the earth-mother, mated with Wakea, the sky-father. From this genealogy came the first kalo, or taro plant, then the first Aliʻi Nui, and then all of the Hawaiian people." Lilikala Kameʻleihiwa, 1991

Eia ua lani a Haloa i pili ai ka hani i ke kapu.

"Here is a chief descended of Haloa, whose kapu makes one hold his breath in dread." Proverb: Paid in compliment, acknowledging long chiefly ancestry, Haloa being one of the most ancient chiefs, only a few generations removed from the gods.

He ʻimi aliʻi, he aliʻi no ke loaʻa; he ʻimi kanaka, he kanaka no ke loaʻa.

"When a chief is sought, a chief is begotten, when a commoner is sought, a commoner is begotten." Proverb: It was a primary responsibility of a chief to seek a mate whose mana would exalt his offspring.

He ʻopu aliʻi.

"Have the heart of an aliʻi." Saying: Have courage, wisdom, compassion, integrity.

A ʻo ka loina nui o na aliʻi Hawaiʻi Nei, ʻo ka haʻahaʻa, ʻo ka ʻoluʻolu, ke aloha a me ka lomomaikaʻi.

"The great customary law of our Hawaiian chiefs was lowliness, courtesy, aloha and inner goodness." Kepelino, c. 1870

O ke aliʻi lilo i ka leʻaleʻa a malama ʻole i ke kanaka me ke kapu akua, ʻamole ia he aliʻi e ku ai i ka moke.

"The chief who is taken with pleasure-seeking and cares not for the welfare of the people or the observation of the kapu of the gods, is not the chief who will become a ruler." Prophesy: Said by Kekuhaupiʻo to Kamehameha.

He aliʻi no ka malu kukui.

"A chief of the kukui shade." Proverb: Said of a chief whose lineage is suspect.

Ua Mau Ke Ea O Ka ʻAina I Ka Pono

"The life of the land is perpetuated in righteousness." The Hawaiʻi State Motto, originally introduced during the reign of Kamehameha III, asserting the sacred links between the Hawaiian people and the land.

Glossary

Before the missionaries created an alphabet for the Hawaiian language, it had not taken a written form. At first, when the language remained in common use, it was written without grammatical guides to pronunciation. As the Native Hawaiian population declined and English became more commonly used, the Hawaiian language fell increasingly into disuse. Because pronunciation might well change the meaning of a word, ʻokina (ʻ), glottal stops, and kahako (ˉ) were introduced to provide a guideline for proper pronunciation and meaning. ʻOkina and kahako have been used throughout the book, except when quoting an original source that does not use them. This select glossary is designed to provide a quick reference for Hawaiian words and names that appear within the chapters that follow:

ʻahuʻula	Long feather cloaks used for royal display.
ʻai kapu	Sacred prohibition against men and women eating together.
ʻāina	The land; carries with it a sense of sacredness, veneration.
aliʻi	Chief, chiefess, noble, royalty.
aliʻi nui	High chief, king.
hale	House; in combination with other words defines specific type of house, i.e., hale moe, or sleeping house.
hānai	Foster child, adopted child; to adopt or serve as provider.
heiau	Temple; ancient site for prayer and religious ceremonies; some were of monumental scale, others quite small and simple.
kāhili	Feather standard; symbol of royalty; usually held by retainers in royal presence.
kāhuna	Class of specialists, as in healing, canoe-building, or martial arts; most commonly used to describe priests who served the pantheon of Hawaiian gods and the aliʻi.
ka mōʻī	The king; title introduced during reign of Kamehameha III.
kapu	Sacred injunctions that defined proper behavior; kapu were in effect in the presence of aliʻi.

kauhale	Royal compound; a cluster of buildings that included men's and women's eating houses, a sleeping house, cooking shed, canoe shed, etc.
kāʻai kapu o Līloa	Sacred feather sash; rare symbol of royalty; included on statue of Kamehameha I at Aliʻiōlani Hale and in Kapaʻau.
kuhina nui	Akin to regent, or prime minister, a political position during the reign of Kamehameha II, III, IV, and V. Eliminated in 1864 with the death of Victoria Kamāmalu.
kuleana	Land title; land granted in Great Māhele of 1848.
lei niho palaoa	Carved bone pendant hung on necklace of plaited human hair as a symbol of royalty. The bone pendant represents the tongue of the god Kū.
māhele	Term used to describe the division of Hawaiian lands in 1848.
mahiole	Feather helmet.
makaʻāinana	Commoners.
makahiki	Ancient annual festival beginning in mid-October at the first sighting of the Pleiades, called makahiki by the Hawaiians; lasting up to four months it is a time for sporting events, hula, and paying tribute to the god Lono and the aliʻi.
mana	Divine power; greatest in those of high aliʻi status, it conferred authority and commanded respect.
mele	Song; chant of any kind; to sing or chant.
moʻo aliʻi	Geneaology of chiefs, history of chiefs, chiefly line of succession.
nīʻaupiʻo	Highest aliʻi rank; offspring of marriage of close blood relatives, e.g., brother and sister, uncle and niece.
pūloʻuloʻu	Kapa covered bail on a stick, used in presence of a chief as a sign of rank; also called kapu stick.

Glossary |

History Makers of the Hawaiian Kingdom

James Blount — U.S. Commissioner sent to Hawai'i by President Grover Cleveland to determine an appropriate U.S. response to the overthrow of the monarchy. His report stated that Lili'uokalani should be restored to the throne.

Sanford Dole (1844–1926) — Missionary-descended, Honolulu-born lawyer who became a prominent reformer; served on Supreme Court; played a prominent role in the overthrow of the monarchy; president of the Republic of Hawai'i; first governor of the Territory.

Walter Murray Gibson (1822–1888) — Prime Minister under Kalākaua; enigmatic personality; worked consistently to maintain Hawai'i's independence; was driven from office and died soon after on the Mainland.

Gerrit P. Judd (1803–1873) — New England-born missionary who joined the government of Kamehameha III; helped convert Hawai'i into a functioning constitutional monarchy; committed to Hawaiian independence.

Ka'ahumanu (c. 1768–1832) — Best-loved wife of Kamehameha I; served as kuhina nui under Kamehameha II, III; played active role in the overthrow of the old gods in 1819.

Kahekili (1713?–1794) — Ali'i nui of Maui. Fought Kalani'ōpu'u and Kamehameha for control of the Hawaiian Islands.

Victoria Ka'iulani (1875–1899) — Niece of Kalākaua and Lili'uokalani. She was named heir to the throne by Lili'uokalani in 1891.

David Kalākaua (1836–1891) — Ali'i elected king in 1874. Played a significant role in restoring pride in Hawaiian tradtions.

Jonah Kūhiō Kalaniana'ole (1871–1922) — Ali'i nephew of Kapi'olani. Named a prince by Kalākaua, he played a significant role following the overthrow of the monarchy, representing Hawai'i in Washington from 1902–1922.

Kalaniʻōpuʻu (c 1740–1782)	Aliʻi nui of the island of Hawaiʻi; father of Kīwalaʻō and Keōua; uncle of Kamehameha I; great grandfather of Kamehameha II, III; named Kamehameha as guardian of war god, Kūkāʻilimoku.
Samuel Kamakau (1815–1876)	Student at Lāhaināluna School in 1830s, his history of ancient Hawaiʻi is a primary source of information on the Hawaiian culture.
Kamehameha I (c. 1753–1819)	Aliʻi who unified Hawaiʻi as a single kingdom. Warrior and ruler of mythic reputation.
Kāne	The procreator, providing fresh water, sunlight and natural abundance. As leading god of the pantheon, he was manifest in more than 70 forms. As Kānehekili he was god of thunder.
Kapiʻolani (1834–1899)	Aliʻi wife of King Kalākaua.
Albert Edward Kauikeaouli (1858–1862)	Na Haku o Hawaiʻi, the Prince of Hawaiʻi. Son of Kamehameha IV and Queen Emma, he died at the age of four.
Kauikeaouli (1813–1854)	High born aliʻi, son of Kamehameha and Keōpūolani; ruled as Kamehameha III from 1824–1853; married to Queen Kalama.
Kaumualiʻi (c. 1780–1824)	Aliʻi nui of Kauaʻi; never defeated in battle by Kamehameha; declared himself subject king to Kamehameha in 1810.
David Kawānanakoa (1868–1908)	Aliʻi nephew of Kapiʻolani, named a prince by Kalākaua; through his offspring the Kawānanakoa line remains current.
Ruth Keʻelikōlani (1826–1883)	Aliʻi great-granddaughter of Kamehameha I; inherited vast tracts of lands which she left to her cousin, Bernice Pauahi.
Mataio Kekūanaoʻa (1794–1868)	Aliʻi who accompanied Kamehameha II to England; married Kīnaʻu, daughter of Kamehameha I; fathered Kamehameha IV and V; served Kamehameha V as minister.
Keōpūolani (1778–1823)	Aliʻi daughter of Kīwalaʻō who was first cousin to Kamehameha I; sacred wife of Kamehameha I; mother of Kamehameha II and III; played an active role in the overthrow of the old gods.
Keōua (c. 1760–1791)	Aliʻi son of Kalaniʻōpuʻu, cousin of Kamehameha; fought for control of the island of Hawaiʻi; defeated in 1791, his body was offered in sacrifice at the dedication of the Puʻukoholā heiau by Kamehameha.
Kīnaʻu (1807–1839)	Aliʻi daughter of Kamehameha; mother of Kamehameha IV and V; kuhina nui under Kamehameha III.

Kīwalaʻō
(c. 1755–1782)
Aliʻi son of Kalaniʻōpuʻu; named by his father to succeed him as aliʻi nui, he was defeated in battle against Kamehameha; his daughter, Keōpūolani, was sacred wife of Kamehameha; grandfather to Kamehameha II and III.

Kūkāʻilimoku
Kū as the god of war; a feather image of Kūkāʻilimoku was left in Kamehameha's keeping by Kalaniʻōpuʻu; Kūkāʻilimoku served as Kamehameha's patron.

Leleiōhoku
(1855–1877)
Aliʻi brother of Kalākaua; adopted by Ruth Keʻelikōlani as heir to the Kamehamehas; named Kalākaua's heir in 1874.

Liholiho
(1796–1824)
High-born aliʻi son of Kamehameha and Keōpūolani; ruled as Kamehameha II from 1819–1824; died in London of measles, as did his wife and half-sister, Kamāmalu.

Alexander Liholiho
(1834–1863)
High-born aliʻi son of Kīnaʻu and Kekūanaoʻa; grandson of Kamehameha, he ruled as Kamehameha IV; married to Queen Emma.

Miriam Likelike
(1851–1887)
Aliʻi sister of David Kalākaua and Liliʻuokalani; mother of Kaʻiulani.

Liliʻuokalani
(1838–1917)
Aliʻi who ruled as Hawaiʻi's last monarch; worked to restore the authority of the crown; forced to abdicate after the monarchy was overthrown on January 17, 1893.

Lono
One of four principal gods of the Hawaiian pantheon; god of fertility, weather, and the harvest; honored each year at makahiki.

Lot Kamehameha
(1830–1872)
Aliʻi grandson of Kamehameha; son of Kīnaʻu and Kekūanaoʻa; ruled from 1863–1872.

Lunalilo
(1835–1874)
Aliʻi who was Hawaiʻi's first elected king; died after little more than one year on the throne.

David Malo
(c. 1793–1853)
Student at Lāhaināluna School; his *Hawaiian Antiquities* is a classic of Hawaiian history and culture.

Bernice Pauahi Bishop
Aliʻi great-granddaughter of Kamehameha; inherited the ancestral Kamehameha land from her cousin, Ruth Keʻelikolani; created a trust used to found and support (1831–1884) the Kamehameha Schools.

Emma Naea Rooke
(1836–1885)
Aliʻi wife of Kamehameha IV. Sought to rule but lost to Kalākaua in a bitter election in 1873.

Robert Wilcox
(1855–1903)
Part-Hawaiian of aliʻi descent; led two insurrections, the first to restore Kalākaua's constitutional powers, the second to restore Liliʻuokalani to the throne; both failed; served as first Hawaiian delegate to the United States Congress after the Territory of Hawaiʻi was declared.

─✶ RULERS OF THE KINGDOM OF HAWAI'I ✶─

KAMEHAMEHA DYNASTY

	Birth	Accession	Death
Kamehameha I	circa 1736	circa 1795	May 8, 1819
Kamehameha II	circa 1797	May 20, 1819	July 4, 1824
Kamehameha III	Aug. 11, 1813	June 6, 1825	Dec. 15, 1854
Kamehameha IV	Feb. 9, 1834	Jan. 11, 1855	Nov. 30, 1863
Kamehameha V	Dec. 11, 1830	Nov. 30, 1863	Dec. 11, 1872

LUNALILO DYNASTY

Lunalilo	Jan. 31, 1832	Jan. 8, 1873	Feb. 3, 1874

KALĀKAUA DYNASTY

David Kalākaua	Nov. 16, 1836	Feb. 12, 1874	Jan. 20, 1891
Lili'uokalani	Sept. 2, 1838	Jan. 29, 1891	Nov. 11, 1917

Monarchy abrogated January 17, 1893.

Provisional Government established January 17, 1893.

Republic of Hawai'i established July 4, 1894.

Hon. Sanford B. Dole named president of Provisional Government of Hawai'i, January 17, 1893; and president of Republic of Hawai'i, July 4, 1894; retains presidency to June 14, 1900.

CHAPTER 1

* A MILLENNIUM OF ISOLATION *

Ancient Hawai'i excites the imagination. Tropic isles of impressive beauty bring to mind a time of purity and innocence. The reality is far more complex and interesting.

Polynesians first arrived almost 2,000 years ago from islands more than 2,000 miles to the south. They brought the traditions and beliefs of their home islands, and today emerge in Hawaiian history as menehune, a smaller people credited with awesome skills at building and of impish reputation. Several centuries later other Polynesians arrived with traditions of their own. Hawaiian oral history begins with their arrival. When migrations from the South Pacific ceased around the thirteenth or fourteenth century, a period of transformation began that saw the emergence of a distinctive Hawaiian culture. During the centuries that followed, the Hawaiians developed a complex cosmology that provided them with a solid spiritual base and a political system that was the most sophisticated and complex in Polynesia. Rocks and plants, humans and animals each possessed life and were descended from the same ancestral spirits. The Polynesians believed all men were descended from gods, but those who could prove it with a sacred genealogy were spiritually elevated. These people were given respect, honor, and power. That ali'i were sacred was a point of faith which was absolute and unchallenged.

Replicas of ancient sculptured ki'i, or god images, stand guard outside the Hale o Keawe at Pu'uhonua o Hōnaunau on the island of Hawai'i. It was here that the bones of dead chiefs, believed to be sacred by Hawaiians, were kept.

During the makahiki season, tribute was paid to the god Lono and to the ali'i. Sporting competitions and hula were part of the festivities, as recorded by British artist John Webber, with the Cook expedition in 1778–1779.

Although very little is known of the first Polynesians to settle in Hawai'i, the later Tahitian settlers brought with them a social and political hierarchy of chiefs. During the long centuries of isolation that followed their arrival, Hawai'i was transformed into an ever more rigidly stratified society.

In ancient Hawai'i, ali'i status was confirmed by mana, and mana was determined by ancestry. The ruling elite was thus drawn from a select group of families with the most powerful bloodlines. The ali'i were supported in their claim to the divine right to rule by a class of specialists called kahuna, acknowledged masters of a variety of trades and skills.

Generation to generation, the system became increasingly complex, isolating the highborn from the common people. All ali'i children received some royal title. As the population grew, so did the number of royal families, primarily from natural increase, but occasionally by the addition of an aliʻi of merit, usually a warrior of great skill or courage who was able to claim the mana of aliʻi rank from his exploits and reputation. It was not impossible for a lower ranked aliʻi to take up arms and gain new status, as Kamehameha had done against his higher-ranked cousin, Kīwalaʻō. Mana was enhanced by powerful deeds.

As with all feudal systems, the aliʻi were responsible for the well-being of the makaʻāinana, or commoners. In return, the makaʻāinana provided labor and a percentage of their output of taro, yams, pigs, sugarcane, feathers (used for royal capes and helmets), wood (for royal canoes, homes, weapons, images, calabashes and more), and a diversity of other goods. This tribute was collected each year during the four months of makahiki, the festival season dedicated to Lono as god of fertility that started in October, when attention was focused on competitive sporting events, feasting, and paying homage to the aliʻi.

In Hawaiʻi, all land belonged to the highest chiefs, not as private property, although their control was absolute, but as stewards for the people and as representatives of the gods. What was expected of a chief in his stewardship of land and people was well-defined. The qualities of leadership included pono, or virtue; malama, caring; kupono, integrity; naʻauao, wisdom; haʻahaʻa, humility; and koa, courage.

While arrogant chiefs might intimidate their people, the system did allow commoners dissatisfied with poor treatment to move to the lands of another

A view of the prosperous village of Waimea, Kauaʻi, as depicted by Webber in 1778.

Webber's view of Kealakekua Bay, island of Hawaiʻi, where Cook would lose his life in 1779, while visiting the Islands for the second time.

Artist Herb Kawainui Kane, Polynesian voyaging authority and Hawaiʻi Island resident, depicts a scene that may have happened as Cook's ship Resolution stood offshore at Kealakekua Bay: A makahiki procession pauses to gaze at the ship with billowing sails. The bearer carries the standard of the god Lono. Similarity of the ship's sails to the Lono standard contributed to the Hawaiians' assumptioin that Cook was Lono, returning.

> hand... ...eth
> Year of Our Reign.
> GOD Save the KING.
>
> *Admiralty-Office, January* 11, 1780.
> CAPTAIN Clerke, of His Majesty's Sloop the Resolution, in a Letter to Mr. Stephens, dated the 8th of June, 1779, in the Harbour of St. Peter and St. Paul, Kamtschatka, which was received Yesterday, gives the melancholy Account of the celebrated Captain Cook, late Commander of that Sloop, with Four of his private Mariners, having been killed on the 14th of February last at the Island of O'why'he, One of a Group of new discovered Islands, in the 22d Degree of North Latitude, in an Affray with a numerous and tumultuous Body of the Natives.
> Captain Clerke adds, that he had received every friendly Supply from the Russian Government; and that as the Companies of the Resolution and her Consort the Discovery were in perfect Health, and the Two Sloops had Twelve Months Stores and Provisions on Board, he was preparing to make another Attempt to explore a Northern Passage to Europe.
>
> *Petersburg, December* 14. Saturday last, being St.

London, January 11, 1780. A newspaper report tells of Cook's death and of "O'why'he, one of a group of newly discovered Islands" in the middle of the Pacific.

ali'i and thereby transfer their allegiance. Successful and respected ali'i were recognized by the size of their following. There might be many dozens in the entourage of one of the highest chiefs. Although women did not frequently rule in ancient Hawai'i or during the Victorian-era monarchy that emerged after contact with the West, they were not without considerable influence and power. In many generations, the highest-born ali'i were women.

Hawaiians venerated their ancestors, so the proper disposal of an ali'i's remains was very important. It was necessary to protect the bones after death, for they retained mana and great harm could come to a family if the bones of the deceased were to fall into the hands of a hostile party.

The arrival of Captain James Cook's expedition in 1778 initiated a transition that dramatically altered Hawaiian society. The first sign of change came with the introduction of foreign weapons and rules of war, with foreigners valued as military advisors to compet-

Artist Herb Kane envisions an impressive and historic scene: Kalani'ōpu'u, ali'i nui of the Island of Hawai'i, welcomes Captain Cook on his arrival in Kealakekua Bay.

A Millennium of Isolation

Two engravings after Webber, 1779, present A fanciful early nineteenth-century view of male and female aliʻi. Many Europeans who first visited Hawaiʻi commented on the appealing looks and healthy vitality of both men and women.

ing chiefs. But it was the start of trade, with the increasing numbers of foreign ships now making Hawaiʻi a port of call, that had an even more fundamental impact. The introduction of a market economy soon undid the traditional relationship between commoners and aliʻi, replacing communal self-sufficiency with an economy based on trade. Farmers were forced to abandon their fields and fishermen to beach their boats to provide the necessary manpower. When that proved inadequate, women and children were also drawn into service.

Trade brought with it the need to deal with the nations from which trade ships set sail. That made foreigners valuable allies for ruling chiefs who could learn from them the ways of the outside world. While the chiefs would continue to serve, first in advisory roles, and later as members of the House of Nobles, their influence would barely survive the nineteenth century, surrendered to forces beyond their control.

Hawaiian historian David Malo described the situation, emphasizing the need to adjust quickly, advising the influential Kīnaʻu, prime minister to Kamehameha III, in a letter that asserted the need to take action to preserve the independence of the kingdom:

> *If a big wave comes in, large fishes will come from the dark Ocean which you never saw before, and when they see the small fishes they will eat them up...The ships of the white man have come, and smart people have arrived from the great countries which you have never seen before, they know our people are few in number and living in a small country; they will eat us up, such has always been the case with large countries, the small ones have been gobbled up...*

Within a generation of the overthrow of the kapu, the aliʻi also fell victim to the demographics of decline, as disease and ennui began to take their toll, killing tens of thousands without regard to status. Once the physical and spiritual links to the land were lost, the class that had stood at the apex of Hawaiian culture, heirs to sixty or more generations as the chants tell it, had been largely reduced to an historic footnote. ■

CHAPTER 2

✴ ROYAL REGALIA ✴

It's not surprising that a society which deified its aliʻi would pamper them in many ways. They enjoyed special foods, feasting on what was forbidden to others. Fishponds stocked with fish solely for the aliʻi lined the coasts of the islands. Chanters recited mele for their pleasure while dancers performed hula, the sensual, sophisticated, ceremonial dance that still serves as a symbol of Hawaiian culture.

Aliʻi houses were larger and more detailed than those of commoners. Although furnishings were minimal as most of life was lived outdoors, household goods such as calabashes, cups, food pounders, tools, and storage gourds were of the finest workmanship.

Talented weavers and Hawaiian craftsmen created objects of aesthetic merit, plaited of hala leaves and sedge. The aliʻi wore the finest cotton-soft kapa, the hand-beaten cloth made from mulberry bark and imprinted with geometric designs. Everyday dress was not elaborate. For royal men, this meant a malo, or loincloth, while royal women wore long, wraparound pāʻū, skirts.

It was, however, through cloaks, capes, and helmets embellished with the brilliant red, yellow, black, and green feathers of rain forest birds, that the highborn were identified. The Hawaiians surpassed all other Pacific Islanders in the variety and quality of their featherwork. The most impressive of these garments were the ʻahuʻula, the wide, floor-length feather cloaks described by Cook's surgeon mate David Samwell, when HMS *Discovery* and *Resolution* dropped anchor in Kealakekua Bay in 1779:

The cloaks are made of fine Netting with red and yellow, feathers curiously worked upon them, these they have of various Lengths, some coming no lower than the Waist & others trailing the Ground. A more rich and elegant Dress than this, perhaps the Arts of Europe, have not yet been able to supply. Inferior Chiefs have Cloaks made of Cock's Tail feathers with a collar of red and yellow…Some again wear yellow Cloth [kapa] in imitation of these Cloaks, which being of very bright Colour appears very well at a distance.

Only the highest ranking nīʻaupiʻo aliʻi were allowed to wear an all-yellow ʻahuʻula, or feather cape. Kamehameha I wore one although of lower rank in order to enhance his prestige. The two hand-held kāhili announced the presence of a highborn chief.

More than sixty years later, a newspaper feature expanded upon this comparison, discussing the prized all-yellow cloak worn by Kamehameha I:

...the value of the cloak would equal that of the purest diamonds in the several European regalia, and including the price of the feathers, not less than a million dollars worth of labor was expended upon it, at the present rate of computing wages.

Fifty-six inches in length and more than twelve feet wide at the base, it is estimated that this impressive cloak (one of fifty-four in collections worldwide, twelve of which are in the Bishop Museum) required the plumage of 80,000 birds. Feathers were collected by maka'ainana as part of their work obligation to their ali'i overlords.

Bird catchers, called kia manu, were trained in the habits of the rain forest birds. Positioned near a likely feeding place, they would attract birds by mimicking their song. Birds were considered a resource, their feathers taken with survival of prized species in mind. The most highly valued yellow feathers came from the mamo and 'ō'ō, both found only on the island of Hawai'i. Their plumage was solid black, with the exception of a few favored yel-

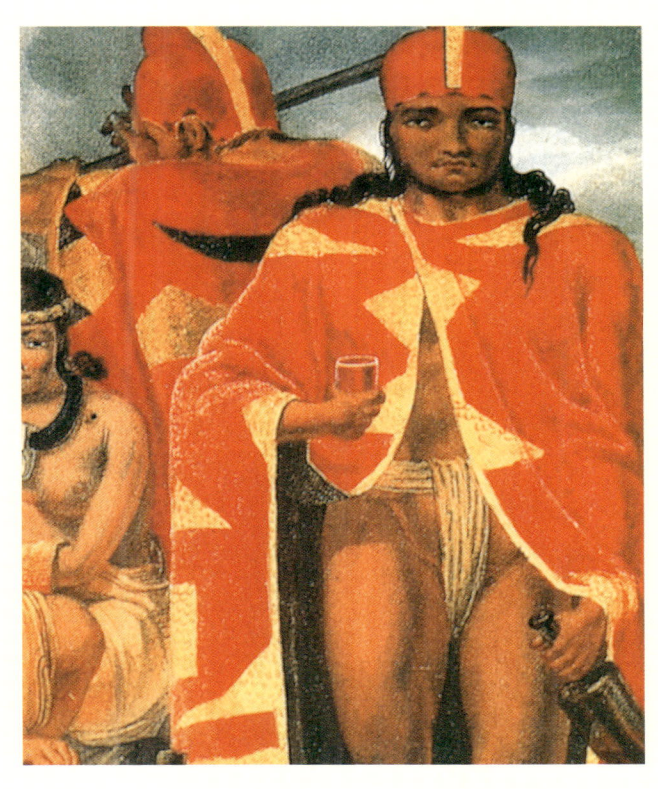

At the direction of Kamehameha I, High Chief Boki, Governor of O'ahu, reprovisions the Russian sloop *Kamchatka*, 1818, and is entertained by Captain Vasilii Golovinin. Ships' artist Mikhail Tikhanov delivers this commanding rendition of the ship's visitors, with the men in splendid examples of Hawai'i's regalia for male chiefs—feathered cloaks, capes, and helmets. The bottle and glass of wine Boki holds testifies to the Western aspect of shipboard entertainment.

The Joy cloak, one of twelve in the Bishop Museum, is the largest of the fifty-four 'ahu'ula still in existence. The red feathers are from the 'i'iwi bird, the yellow feathers from the 'ō'ō and mamo bird.

(Left) 'Ō'ō birds provided one source of yellow feathers, while the 'i'iwi (below) was source for red feathers for a variety of featherwork. After the 'ō'ō were harvested they were released. The 'i'iwi were killed for their plumage and then usually eaten. Feathers of various colors and sizes came from forest birds, domestic fowl, and seabirds, captured in many ways (by snares, bird lime, nets, stoning, and other devices) by professional bird hunters (po'e hahai manu; kia manu).

7 | Royal Regalia

Turning his attention to helmet detail, artist Mikhail Tikhanov, aboard the Kamchatka, 1818, renders two views of Boki's tight-fitting, elaborately structured feather helmet (mahiole)—full frontal and profile—and, at Boki's right, shows Chief Kahekili (commander of the Hawaiian navy) wearing a helmet of different design.

(Right) A modern replica of a feather helmet (mahiole). For better or worse, when used in battle, the mahiole served as a means of identification.

low feathers clustered near the wings and tail. These were plucked and the birds released for a future harvest. Other birds, like the 'i'iwi, which provided the red-orange feathers that were most commonly used, were sacrificed, since choice feathers covered most of their bodies. Most of these birds are now extinct, victims of introduced diseases and species, and the destruction of habitat. The fine netting to which the feathers were attached was made of the olonā, a shrub likely brought to Hawai'i by the Polynesians. It was cultivated in the forests and harvested after a year's growth. The stalks were then stripped into fibers used to weave a netting to which the individual feathers could be tied.

Feathers were also used to ornament the mahiole, the distinctively shaped helmets worn by ali'i at ceremonial events and in battle. In making a helmet, a tough, protective framework was woven from the aerial rootlets of the 'ie'ie vine. Feathers or human hair were tied to the frame with olonā threads. As with the dense netting of feathered cloaks, capes, and aprons, the framework of the mahiole was designed to provide protection in battle.

Perhaps the rarest symbol of royal power was the long sash that was draped over the shoulder and wrapped around the waist. One called kā'ai kapu o Līloa, "the sacred sash of Līloa," is at the Bishop

Statue on the Island of Hawai'i shows Kamehameha I garbed in replicas of royal raiment, including mahiole (helmet), 'ahu'ula (cloak), and ka ai ka pu o Liloa (feather sash held sacred).

Royal Regalia | *8*

Museum. Nearly twelve-feet long and covered with feathers on both sides, it is partially edged with rows of fish teeth and teeth of ali'i defeated in battle, which added to its mana. The sash was reputedly made on the order of Līloa, a king of mythic reputation, for his son 'Umi in 1475. It was used in the investiture of Big Island high chiefs from 'Umi to Kamehameha II.

Feathers were used in several other important symbols of royal status. The 'ō'ō, which provided soft yellow feathers for capes and helmets, also supplied the long, shiny black feathers that were favored in the kāhili, the tall standards that accompanied ali'i during their travels, carried by young noblemen related to the honored ali'i. Their handles might be ornamented with carved tortoise shell or human bone. One particularly unique kāhili in the Bishop Museum includes bones from twelve high chiefs killed in the battle of Nu'uanu in 1795, when Kamehameha the Great defeated Kalanikūpule and gained control of O'ahu. By including the bones of rival chiefs, this kāhili enhanced Kamehameha's mana.

Feather decoration was also incorporated into kapu wands, pointed wooden sticks with tops decorated with feathers or dog hair. These were spiked into the ground around the perimeter of a field, or around dwellings, to indicate that the area was kapu, or off-limits. Pūlo'ulo'u, or kapu sticks, typically four- or five-feet long and topped with a ball of white kapa, were carried in advance of an ali'i processional to announce the presence of a kapu chief to those of lesser rank. They might also be posted outside a dwelling when a kapu chief was in residence. With the exception of feather neck lei, called lei hulu manu, to identify female ali'i, feathered regalia were worn only by the men. Other female regalia included rings and bracelets of turtle shell and bone, called kupe'e. Both men and women of high rank wore a lei niho palaoa. Consisting of a hooked ivory pendant hung on braided human hair, the distinctive necklace was part of the regalia that identified ali'i.

When the kapu were broken and the old order collapsed in 1819, transforming the structure of Hawaiian society, the use of ancient regalia declined. Feather cloaks and capes were retained as symbols of the past by those who followed Kamehameha on the throne, but by the 1830s none of the feathered regalia were any longer in use, except for feather leis and kāhili. The ali'i, in fact, were the first to adopt Western dress, starting with Kamehameha I, who posed for a portrait wearing a shirt and trousers.

Kamehameha II introduced the military uniforms that also appealed to his successors. Ali'i women were soon dressed from the neck down in the style of missionary respectability. Influenced by foreign-born advisers, Hawai'i's kings sought to project a "civilized" appearance consistent with the expecta-

In pageantry, a twenty-first century Hawaiian honors ancient cultural traditions, portraying here a chiefess of high rank. This is evidenced by her neck piece, a hook pendant hung on braided human hair. An accessory of rank common to men and women, it was made in various sizes and from a variety of materials. This replica recalls the lei niho palaoa, with pendant carved of whale tooth ivory.

This short feathered cape, in Bishop Museum (Honolulu, Hawai'i), was once worn by Kauai'i's King Kaumuali'i.

9 | Royal Regalia

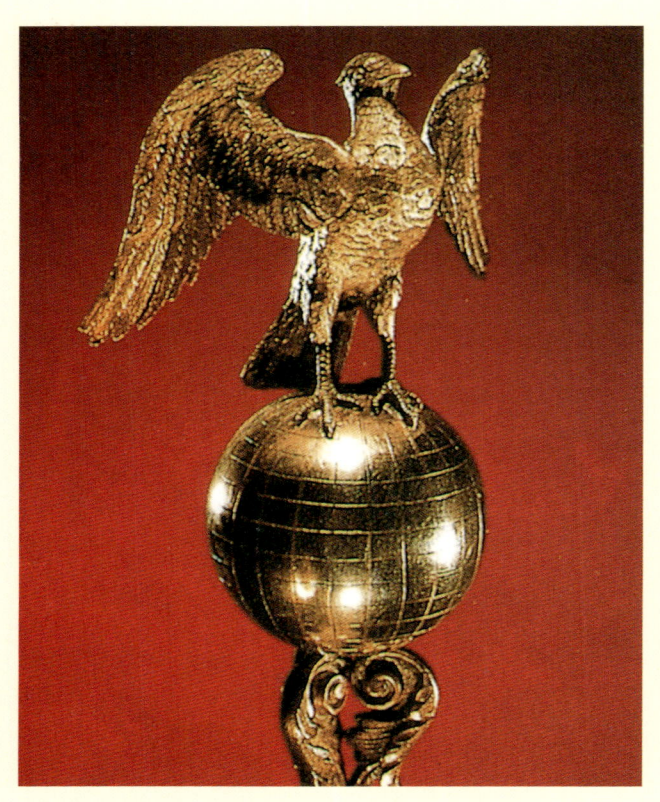

A dove sits atop a globe in the Royal Scepter created for King Kalākaua's coronation in 1883.

The Ring of State was placed on Kalākaua's finger at his coronation as ensign of kingly dignity.

tions of Westerners. From princely titles to medals and uniforms, the trappings of royalty acknowledged new influences. By the time of Kamehameha III's reign (1825–1854), the Hawaiian monarchy had taken on a decidedly Victorian look, influenced by a royal predisposition toward things British. Uniforms complete with gold braid replaced feathered cloaks, while a crown replaced the feathered mahiole on the head of the aliʻi nui, now called ka mōʻī, or king. A cross was far more likely to be found around a royal neck than was a lei niho palaoa.

For royal women, the nineteenth century was also a time to adapt to new standards. The topless pāʻū was replaced by the neck-to-ankles modesty of Victorian fashion. Handmade kapa was cast aside in favor of loomed silks from China and cottons imported from America. When King Kalākaua (1874–1891) completed the transformation from a Polynesian to a Victorian kingdom, royal medals were struck, a new coat of arms drawn, and a scepter, sword, ring, and crown were introduced as royal symbols. Kalākaua's efforts culminated in a coronation ceremony held in 1883 on the grounds of ʻIolani Palace. Completed one year earlier, it replaced the far simpler residences of preceding kings just as the coronation replaced the ceremonies of Polynesian times. The celebrations, timed to coincide with the ninth anniversary of Kalākaua's election to the throne, cost $50,000. With consular representatives of several nations in attendance and U.S. and French warships anchored offshore, the culturally hybrid ceremony began. Following a choral rendering of *"Almighty Father, Hear! The Isles do Wait on Thee,"* the king's titles were announced. Then he was presented with the ancient Hawaiian regalia, the pūloʻuloʻu (kapu stick), palaoa (ivory hook), and kāhili (feather standard), by Poʻomaikelani, sister of the queen. Kalākaua then received a sword, a magnificent feather cloak, a royal ring, and a scepter; all symbols of his kingly authority. Kalākaua's nephews, the princes Kūhiō and Kawānanakoa, made a formal entrance carrying two newly made crowns on velvet cushions. The king then lifted one crown and, in Napoleonic fashion, placed it on his head. Taking the second crown, he turned to Kapiʻolani and placed it on her head, saying, *"I place this crown upon your head, to share the honors of my throne."* The royal couple knelt to receive the blessings of the household chaplain, then rose and

Royal Regalia | 10

returned to the palace while the Royal Hawaiian Band played.

The two weeks that followed saw a series of ceremonial events, including a sailing regatta, a display of fireworks, nightly performances of hula and the dedication of an American-designed, Italian-cast bronze statue of Kamehameha I. Coronation festivities culminated in a grand lūʻau for an estimated 5,000 guests that was favorably covered in the *Pacific Commercial Advertiser*. To others, mainly resident foreigners and missionary-descended businessmen, the fortnight of activities generated much negative comment. The Planters' *Monthly,* a trade journal of plantation agriculture hostile to Kalākaua's rule, expressed attitudes that were soon to surface with increasing frequency:

> *The so-called Coronation of the King, with all the attendant follies and extravagances has been directly damaging to the property interests and welfare of the country. It has been demoralizing in its influence, and productive of only harm... For the furtherance of the Coronation public measures of pressing importance have been neglected* [the hula dancers were] *a retrograde step of heathenism and a disgrace to the age.*

The regalia displayed at the coronation, an eclectic blend of traditionally Hawaiian and imperially European elements, could not alter the course of events. Within ten years of Kalākaua's coronation, the monarchy was overthrown. The royal regalia, of both Hawaiian and foreign inspiration, would prove to be little more than reminders of an era that had surrendered to events which Hawaiʻi's once-divine aliʻi could no longer dominate. ■

(Top) King Kalākaua's crown, crafted of gold and gemstones for his coronation, is now in ʻIolani Palace. By the mid nineteenth century, much of Hawaiʻi's royal regalia mirrored European models. (Bottom) Created by Kamehameha V, the Order of Kamehameha was bestowed on foreign dignitaries and loyal subjects.

11 | Royal Regalia

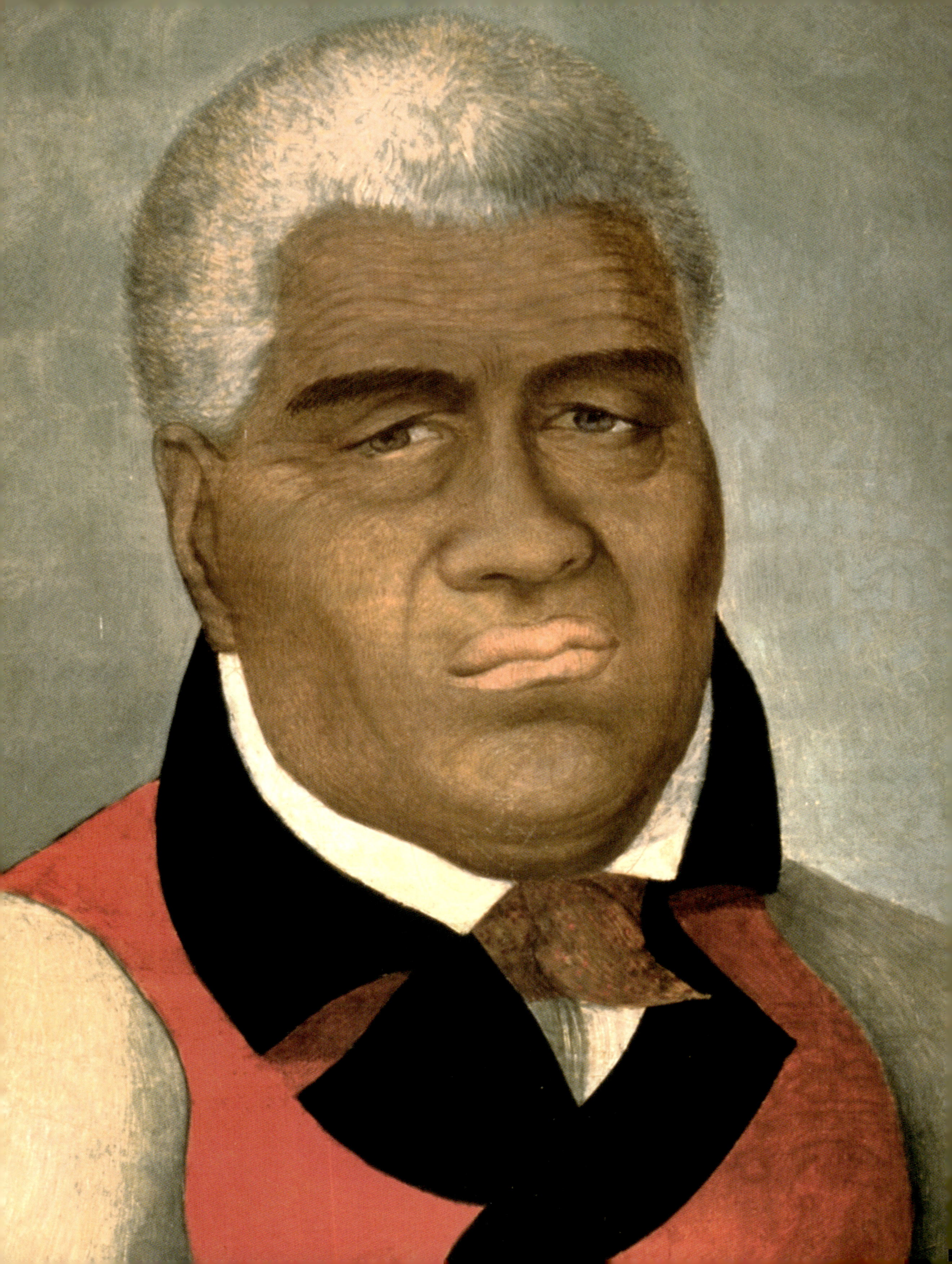

CHAPTER 3

KAMEHAMEHA
The Warrior King (1795-1819)

Named the lonely one, Kamehameha was fated to play destiny's role as the first and greatest of Hawai'i's kings. Born into the traditions of Polynesian Hawai'i, where centuries-old customs remained unchallenged, he would die with the old ways on the verge of collapse. While the kingdom he had created would last for most of the nineteenth century, the Hawai'i of his youth would survive his death by less than a month.

It is known that he was born in the Kohala district, near the northernmost tip of the island of Hawai'i around 1750. It is said that when he was born, a comet blazed across the night sky, an omen of his ultimate rise to power. His mother was Kekuiapoiwa, a Kona chiefess. His father was Keōua Kupuapā Kalaninui, though some believe he was the son of King Kahekili of Maui.

It was foretold in priestly dreams that he would ultimately challenge the rule of the ali'i nui, Alapa'i, so his life was in jeopardy from the moment of birth. He was quickly removed from his mother by a chief named Nae'ole, who then took him into hiding, raising the young ali'i for the first years of his life. At the age of five, after Alapa'i's death, Kamehameha was taken into the royal court by the new ali'i nui, his uncle Kalani'ōpu'u. Here he received the training accorded a high-ranking ali'i and quickly established a reputation as a skilled warrior that was confirmed many times in a life filled with combat. In his early teens, Kamehameha was said to have moved the Naha Stone, fulfilling a prophecy that the man who could move this great monolith, cut for the tomb of the legendary fifteenth-century ali'i, 'Umi, would ultimately unite the islands.

More stylized than documentary, only a few contemporary pictures of Kamehameha exist, paintings by European artists employed on round-the-world voyages of science and exploration. He is described as handsome and impressively built, standing six-feet-six-inches tall

The diary of Vasili Golovnin, captain of the Russian ship *Kamchatka* that reached Hawai'i in 1818, reveals a sense of Kamehameha one year before his death, when age and Western influence had already had an impact:

He was dressed in European fashion, but very simply...[in] light green velvet trousers, a white shirt, a silk kerchief around his neck, a coffee brown silk vest, white stockings and shoes, and a soft felt hat. Tameamea [Kamehameha] is already very old; he claims to be seventy-nine. However, he is alert, strong, active, temperate and sober, never takes strong drink, and eats moderately. In him one observes a most amazing mixture of childish behavior and ripe judgment and actions that would not disgrace even a European ruler. His honesty and love of justice are demonstrated by his behavior.

Kamehameha was already settled in Kailua-Kona when artist Louis Choris, who accompanied Captain Otto von Kotzebue on the Russian ship *Rurick*, painted this intriguing picture of the aging king in 1816. A later version (left) has the king dressed in Western garb.

The 'Ahu'ena heiau at Kamakahonu, Kamehameha's royal compound in Kailua-Kona, in an early nineteenth century view by Louis Choris.

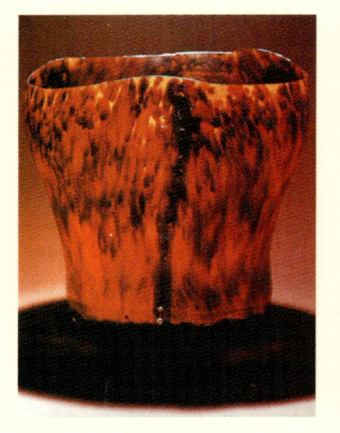

(Above) The beautifully crafted tortoise shell medicine bowl and ivory medicine pounder used by Kamehameha I. (Right) The feather-image of Kūkā'ilimoku, now in the Bishop Museum, had been placed under Kamehameha's protection Kalani'ōpu'u, his uncle and ali'i nui of the Island of Hawai'i.

Timing played a critical role in Kamehameha's rise to power. As he reached manhood, a multi-island Hawaiian kingdom became the political goal of the most powerful chiefs, with his royal relatives already at war with that objective in mind. When Captain Cook arrived in 1778, Kamehameha took notice of the English weaponry. In his mid-twenties at the time, Kamehameha was intrigued and impressed with Western technology. His forces eventually captured a schooner, the *Fair American*, taking on two seamen, Isaac Davis and John Young, as advisers.

As a nephew of Kalani'ōpu'u, Kamehameha was not in direct line to succeed as ali'i nui of the island of Hawai'i when his uncle died in 1781. Kamehameha's claim led first to civil war on the Big Island, then to battles with chiefs on other islands, most notably, Kahekili of Maui. Having been told by the kahuna Kapoukahi that victory would follow the construction of a heiau dedicated to Kū at Pu'ukoholā, Kamehameha committed his forces to the construction of the largest and last of the great temples built to the old gods.

With Maui and the Big Island under his control, Kamehameha trained his sights on O'ahu. Abraham Fornander, writing in the 1860s about the final battle at the Nu'uanu Pali, describes the scene:

At Puiwa the hostile forces met, and for a while the victory was hotly contested, but the superiority, of Kamehameha's artillery, the number of his guns, and the better practice of his soldiers, soon turned the day in his favor, and the defeat of the Oahu forces became an accelerated rout and a promiscuous slaughter.

Of those who were not killed... a large number were driven over the pali at Nuuanu, a precipice several hundred feet in height, and perished miserably. Kalanikupule was hotly pursued...finally he was captured... killed, brought to Kamehameha, and sacrificed to the war god Kuka-ilimoku.

Kamehameha was now the ruler of a multi-island kingdom. Only Kaua'i remained out of his grasp. The first attempt at invasion was thwarted by a storm, the second by a plague that devastated his troops. While Kaua'i

Kamehameha | 14

Artist Herb Kane portrays Kamehameha I on one of his enormous peleleu (war canoes), designed specifically for conquest. It is likely some peleleu carried more than one hundred men. Although basically a Hawaiian canoe, peleleu incorporated some Western ship design elements. Note mounted swivel gun.

would never be conquered, it would join the Hawaiian Kingdom by agreement.

Kamehameha mellowed in the decades that followed his failure to conquer Kaua'i. Seeing the suffering resulting from arbitrary use of chiefly power and years of uninterrupted warfare, he tried to modify the impact of war on innocents caught in the midst of civil conflict. The story is told of how Kamehameha instituted what came to be called the Law of the Splintered Paddle, designed to protect the weak from the strong. As a young warrior, Kamehameha had been involved in a raid on a fishing village in Puna, a district under the rule of a rival ali'i. One defender attacked Kamehameha, whose foot had become wedged in a lava-rock crevice, hitting him with a canoe paddle that splintered from the blow. Kamehameha survived the attack, but long remembered its

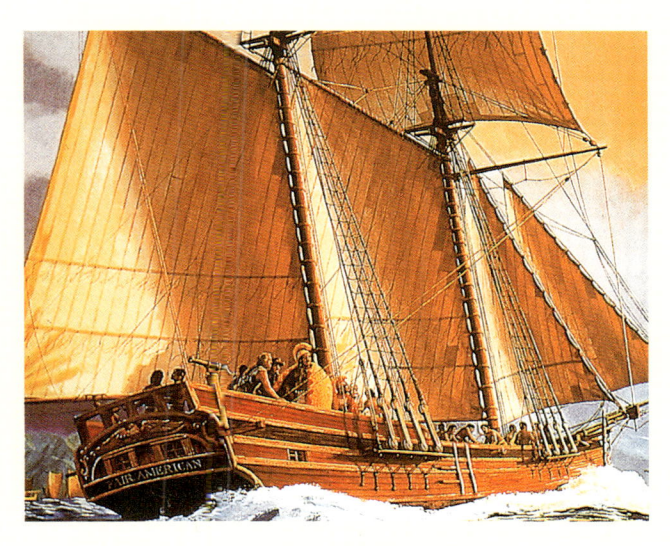

Kamehameha aboard the captured *Fair American*. Making use of Western weapons and tactics gave him a decisive advantage over his rivals. From the capture of the *Fair American*, Kamehameha gained the services of seamen John Young and Isaac Davis.

15 | Kamehameha

In Herb Kane's painting commemorating one of ancient Hawai'i's seminal events, a full moon rises over the newly completed Pu'ukoholā, a vast heiau beuilt in 1790, by Kamehameha I for his war god, Kūkā'ilimoku, to fulfill a priestly prediction that this would pave the way for unification of the Islands under Kamehameha's rule. Within five years, Kamehameha had created a multi-island kingdom.

Kamehameha's forces landed on O'ahu in 1795, in an effort to wrest control of the Island from Kalanikūpule, heir of Maui ali'i nui Kahekili. Although Kalanikūpule escaped, his warriors were forced into retreat, and many were pushed over the precipice at Nu'uanu Pali. Kane depiction.

impact. Years later he issued an edict that protected women, children, the old, and the infirm from arbitrary attack.

In 1812, Kamehameha moved his court from Waikīkī to Kailua-Kona on the island of Hawaiʻi. In his sixties, survivor of battles, intrigues and a lifetime provoking turmoil and change, he was now ready to return to his roots and the timeless Hawaiʻi of his ancestors. The kingdom he had fought for was now at peace. His mana had been confirmed by acts of heroism and victory.

Now trade was bringing with it the first hint of prosperity as it was defined by the outside world. The world beyond the horizon still represented more of a challenge than a threat, although Kamehameha undoubtedly understood that difficult times lay ahead. More than a chief, Kamehameha was the definitive aliʻi, the embodiment of a way of life. Even after he died in May of 1819, attended by Kaʻahumanu and the royal offspring he'd fathered with Keōpūolani, it was his mana that gave legitimacy to the monarchy that followed. Today, nearly 200 years after his passing, he still inspires, his life and deeds now legendary. ■

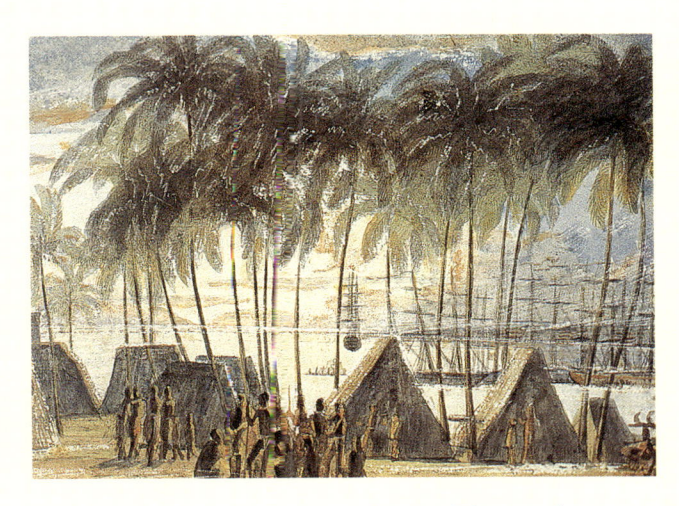

The forest of masts offshore reveals Honolulu as an important port in this 1816 view by Louis Choris.

Artist Herb Kane imagines an exchange between the aging Kamehameha and his son and successor, Liholiho, at the royal compound at Kailua-Kona where Kamehameha would die, 1819.

Kamehameha

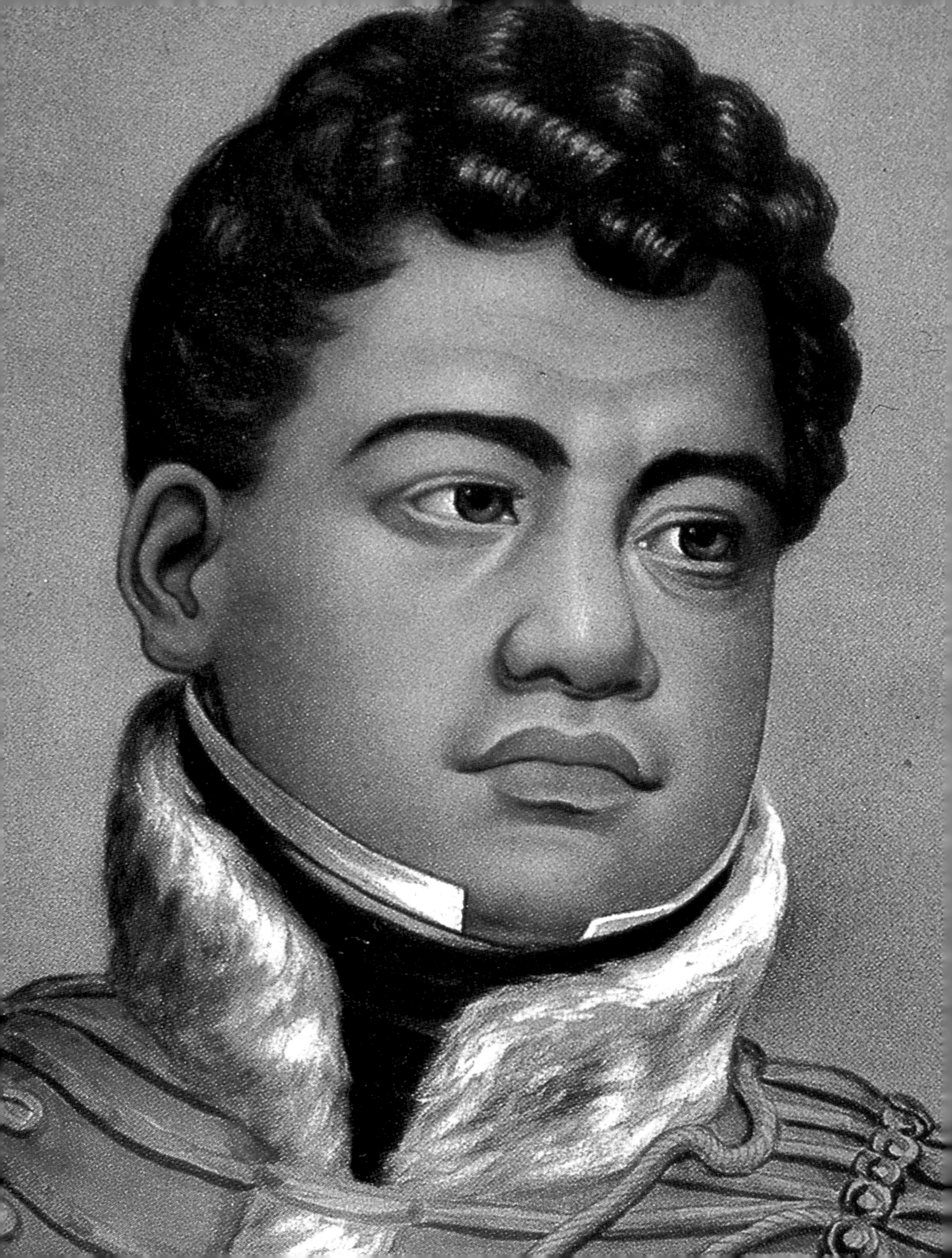

CHAPTER 4

LIHOLIHO / KAMEHAMEHA II
Sailing in New Seas (1819–1824)

The first-born of Kamehameha and Keōpūolani was destined for Hawai'i's throne. Indulged as a child for his sacred mana, he grew to manhood under the care of Ka'ahumanu, his father's favorite wife. Reared in the traditional Hawaiian ways by Kamehameha, his priests, and a council of experts in cultural and practical matters, Liholiho was being trained to rule a kingdom that had been transformed by contact with the outside world. At his installation, Ka'ahumanu proclaimed herself his equal:

Hear me, O Divine one [Liholiho], for I make known to you the will of your father. Behold these chiefs and the men of your father and these your guns, and this your land, but you and I shall share the realm together.

Whether or not Kamehameha had actually granted Ka'ahumanu such extensive power, it was obvious that she was determined to influence the twenty-three-year-old king. Liholiho was as confused as other young Hawaiians growing up without the spiritual and social certainty that had existed for preceding generations. While Kamehameha I lived, the old order had been maintained, his moral authority preserving the status quo even though it was obvious that substantial change was unavoidable.

Queen Kamāmalu, favorite wife of Kamehameha II, pictured before and during their 1824 trip to London, where both died of measles within six days of each other.

From the start, Liholiho was confronted by domestic and foreign challenges. Tensions were building between those who favored change and those who wished to preserve the traditional ways. Discontent first surfaced among the older, more conservative ali'i. Dissatisfied with the distribution of lands that followed the death of Kamehameha I, they pressed Liholiho to redistribute crown lands and to share the substantial profits generated by royal trade monopolies.

Freed of Kamehameha's firm grip on power, Ka'ahumanu and Keōpūolani, the two most powerful of Kamehameha's widows and ali'i of high rank in their own right, soon began to pursue radical change. They sought to discredit the kapu system that regulated every part of life in Hawai'i, in particular, the 'ai kapu, which forbade men and women from eating together, and forbade women from eating pork, bananas, and other foods.

In Liholiho's presence, Ka'ahumanu partook of foods forbidden to women. Keōpūolani followed suit several days later, breaking the 'ai kapu by lunching on bananas and pork in the presence of both Liholiho and her younger son, Kauikeaouli. Unnerved by these events, Liholiho withdrew from Kailua to Kawaihae. Here tradition-minded ali'i gathered,

(Opposite) King Kamehameha II (Liholiho), in fur-trimmed finery. Watercolor by unknown artist, thought to be bsed on lithography by J. Hayter, London, 1824.

Honolulu in 1821, in a watercolor attributed to American C. E. Bensell. The newly built fort is visible in the center, surrounded by traditional thatch houses. The building to the right with the peaked roof is the first Kawaiaha'o Church.

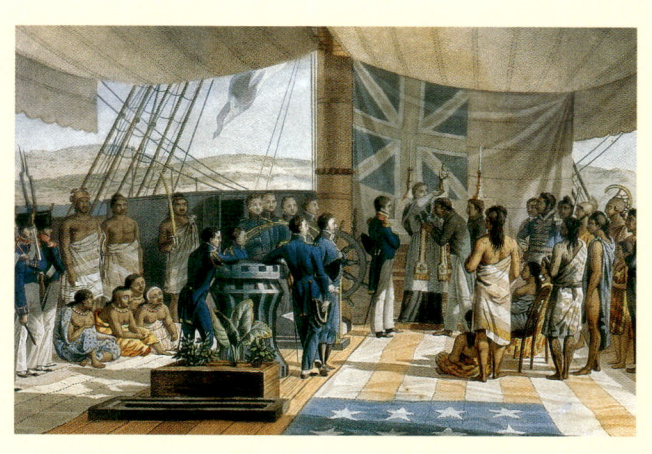

Although Kamehameha came to power with the support of the gods of Polynesia, the old order was on the verge of collapse by the end of his reign. After Kamehameha's death, his advisor, Kalanimōkū, was baptized aboard the French ship *L'Uranie* in a ceremony attended by Kamehameha II, Ka'ahumanu, and Kauikeaouli, the king's younger brother. Kalanimōkū was the first Hawaiian to be baptized. By the mid-1820s, American missionaries had converted many ali'i to Christianity. They sought to secure the favor of the new God and benefit from the education the missionaries provided. After sketches by Jacques Arago, aboard L'Uranie, off Kawaiahe, 1819.

demanding that the twenty-three-year-old king reaffirm the kapu system and deal firmly with the offending dowager queens.

Ka'ahumanu continued to influence Liholiho. Finally, during a great feast during the makahiki season in November 1819, Liholiho rose from his seat and made his way to the women's table. In full view of the expectant crowd he sat down and began to eat. A royal decree confirmed an end to the authority of the kapu. There was to be no turning back. Liholiho's actions immediately put in question the very structure of Hawaiian society. Within a week, the worst fears of those resisting Liholiho's actions were confirmed, when Ka'ahumanu, acting as kuhina nui, ordered the destruction of all the ancient heiau and their host of once-feared gods. Rebellion briefly followed but was quickly quelled by the king's forces.

After his defeat of the tradition-minded chiefs, Liholiho was soon forced to deal with the demands of the foreign-born community for favorable treatment, commercial privileges, trade concessions and land, forcing the king to reevaluate just how far to go to satisfy them.

Even more disturbing were the growing number of whalers and trade ships making port calls in the islands each year. Free of the inhibitions that might have restrained them in more familiar places, sailors frequented the bars and brothels that had sprung up in the ports of Honolulu and Lāhainā. Aside from loud, often aggressive behavior, they brought with them diseases that would soon decimate the Hawaiian population—chicken pox, smallpox, bubonic plague, typhoid, venereal diseases, and other lethal illnesses. To better monitor events, Kamehameha II moved his capital from the island of Hawai'i to Maui. For the next few years he traveled throughout the islands, escaping difficulties ashore with long sails aboard the *Ha'aheo o 'Hawai'i* (Pride of Hawai'i), a brig purchased for $90,000 from revenues accrued by selling shiploads of sandalwood.

It was during Liholiho's reign that the first missionaries arrived, just as the kapu were being overthrown and the heiau destroyed. The first American missionaries had departed New Bedford, Massachusetts, on an eight-month voyage to what was then called the Sandwich Islands. The *Thaddeus* reached Kealakekua Bay on the island of Hawai'i in April 1820. The process of converting the Hawaiians to Christianity was simplified by the spiritual void created by the collapse of the old religion. Although the old ways lingered, particularly in the countryside where family gods were worshipped in private, the ali'i set the standard, becoming the first Christian converts.

Liholiho, fearing foreign influence on his island nation, decided to sail to Great Britain to procure King George IV's protection for Hawai'i. Leaving Ka'ahumanu empowered as regent, with Kalanimōkū to administer in his name, Liholiho departed, accompanied by his favorite wife, Kamāmalu, high chief Boki, governor of O'ahu, and Boki's wife Liliha. After seven months at sea, they arrived in England. Their portraits were painted, and their visit was well-covered by the press. At a meeting scheduled with King George IV, Liholiho was planning to affirm his father's request for a British protectorate over the Hawaiian Islands. Before the meeting occurred, Liholiho and Kamāmalu came down with measles. Neither had the immunities to fight off a disease that had not existed in Hawai'i before the coming of the Europeans. Measles led to pneumonia and on July 8, 1824, Kamāmalu died. Liholiho, already bedridden, despaired at the news, lapsed into a coma, and passed away six days later. When H.M.S *Blonde*, a forty-six-gun naval frigate, set sail from Portsmouth bound for Hawai'i some weeks later, it carried the bodies of Liholiho and Kamāmalu, along with the members of the royal party. Far from home, without proper priestly counsel, the ancient rituals that followed death were ignored. Even after their bodies reached Hawai'i their bones were not removed and hidden as tradition dictated.

The four years of Liholiho's brief reign bridged two epochs. It would remain for those who followed to deal with the problems that accompanied contact with the outside world. ■

In 1823 Kamehameha II and Queen Kamāmalu sailed for England, where they were royally entertained and attended a performance at London's Drury Lane Theatre. John William Gear lithograph, 1824.

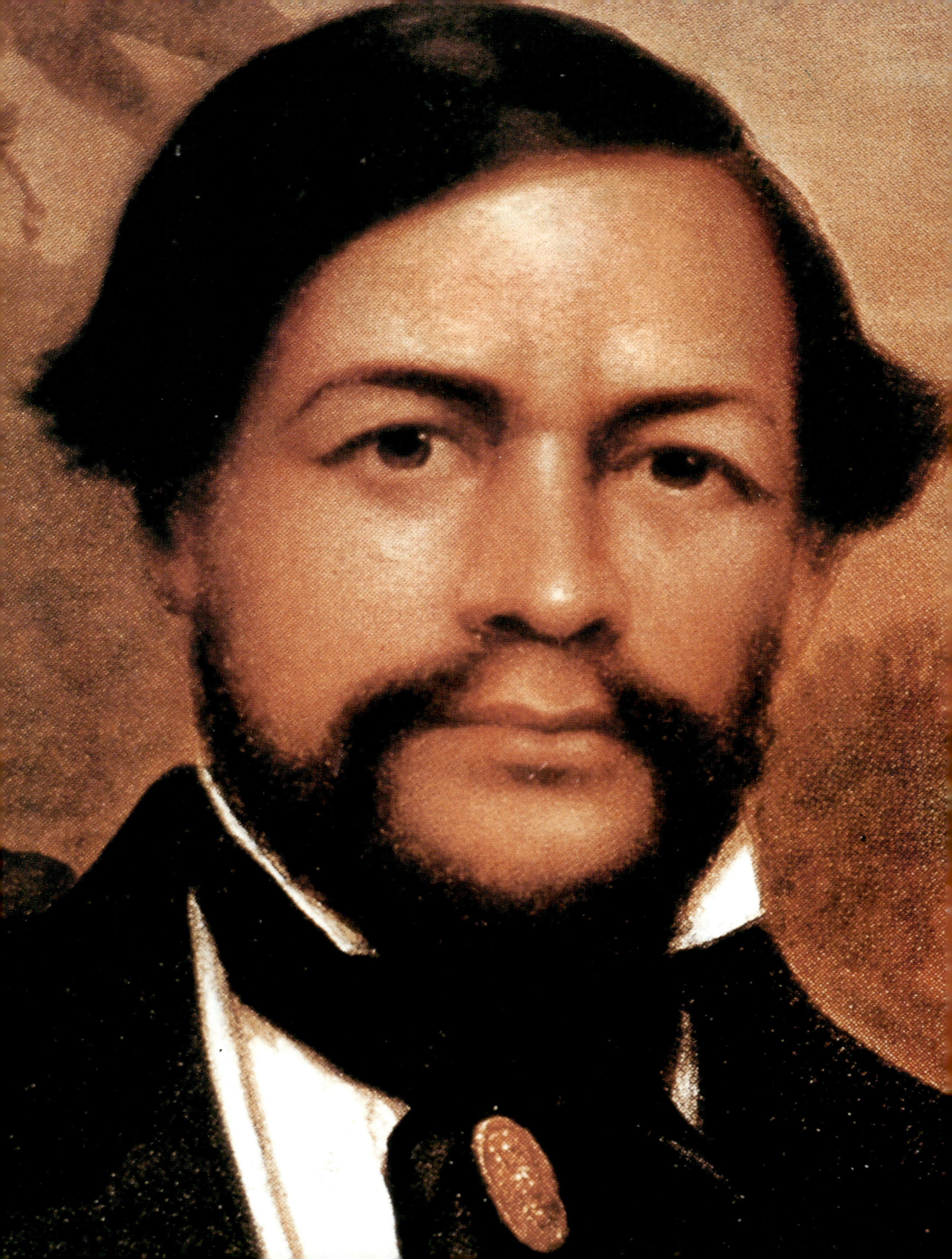

CHAPTER 5

KAUIKEAOULI / KAMEHAMEHA III
King of the Sandwich Isles (1825–1854)

On March 17, 1814, in Keauhou on the Kona coast of the island of Hawai'i, Queen Keōpūolani bore Kamehameha a second son. Named Kauikeaouli, this child of Kamehameha's old age was seventeen years younger than his brother, Liholiho. While Liholiho grew up with the traditions of the past intact, most of Kauikeaouli's childhood followed the collapse of the old order. Heir to a warrior's kingdom, his frame of reference was not formed by great victories, but by a world in which Hawai'i was becoming a pawn of foreigners. During Kauikeaouli's thirty-year reign as Kamehameha III, the longest of Hawai'i's eight monarchs, Hawai'i moved from a feudal theocracy to a constitutional monarchy, with a sophisticated ministerial government.

Kauikeaouli's reign began early in 1825, several months after the tragic deaths in London of Kamehameha II and Queen Kamāmalu. Still a child when he came to the throne, Kauikeaouli was guided through the first years of his reign by members of his father's court. Foremost were the warrior chief Kalanimōkū and the dowager queen Ka'ahumanu.

Serving as kuhina nui, Ka'ahumanu was the real power behind the throne until she died in 1832, when Kamehameha III was seventeen. The young king's half-sister, Kīna'u, was then named kuhina nui, providing the still inexperienced king with an advisor for the next five years of his reign. It was not until Kīna'u's death in 1839 that Kamehameha III was free to rule on his own. Yet his freedom to act unilaterally was soon compromised by circumstances beyond his control.

Kauikeaouli, King Kamehameha III, and consort, Queen Kālama. Also known as Hakaleleponi Kapakuhaili, Kālama was the daughter of Naihekukui, a minor chief and officer of Kamehameha I's navy. The couple was married by the Reverend Hiram Bingham in February 1837, beginning the longest of any Hawaiian reign. Kālama, a woman of business and financial management acumen, became a wealthy woman by the time of her death, 1870.

While the king resisted Christian teachings, the new religion made steady progress with both ali'i and commoners, offering the promise of spiritual salvation at a time of uncertainty. The technological superiority of Western culture and the ability of foreigners to resist diseases that were decimating the Hawaiians seemed proof of the overwhelming power of the Western God. The missionaries taught the Hawaiians a theology that alienated them from their cultural roots as it tried to prepare them for

In 1825, eleven-year-old Kauikeaouli, pictured in a portrait by British artist Robert Dampier, was named King Kamehameha III.

A daguerreotype of Kamehameha III, c. 1850-1854.

the future. The process was accelerated by the missionaries' creation of a written Hawaiian language between 1822 and 1826.

The introduction of writing and a system of universal education were culturally significant. In the Hawai'i of old, where knowledge was considered a manifestation of mana, words were considered sacred. With the democratization of knowledge, Hawaiian culture moved another large step further from its roots. Equally destructive of traditional values and culture were missionary efforts at providing the Hawaiians with a secular education.

The first missionary schools had opened in the early 1820s. By 1831, there were numerous schools in the Islands, with an enrollment of more than 50,000 students, the majority being adults. Two schools were of particular importance in the process of educating Hawaiians in Western technology and belief. The first opened in 1831 in Lāhainā, where Kamehameha III initially held court. Named Lāhaināluna Seminary, it printed many of the first editions of primers, textbooks, and Bibles for Native scholars. Its presses also printed Hawai'i's first money, and published books of lasting significance on Hawaiian history and culture by Samuel Kamakau, David Malo, and others. Through their efforts much of what we know of the Hawaiian past was preserved.

The second school, called the Chiefs' Children's School in recognition of its ali'i enrollment, opened in Honolulu in 1839 at royal request. Five of Hawai'i's future monarchs were educated here by former missionaries Amos and Juliette Cooke. In 1840, a law was enacted providing for a national system of common schools under government auspices. From that point on, missionary influence began to wane. Through them the groundwork had been laid, with the Hawaiian people among the most literate in the world.

By the 1830s, hundreds of ships were making port calls in Hawai'i each year. Trade ships, warships, and whalers brought with them money for reprovisioning and providing ship-weary sailors with the pleasures of shore leave. The sailor's life appealed to Hawaiians, many of whom were quite ready to sign on as crew members. So many shipped out that Kamehameha III sponsored a law forbidding Hawaiians from signing on with foreign ships. Trade brought more settlers to the islands, with entrepreneurial foreigners soon requesting lands on which to establish businesses that included ranches and plantations. The first plantation, started in 1835, was a thousand-acre tract granted to Ladd & Company at Kōloa, Kauaʻi, for an annual rent of $300. When Kamehameha III died in 1854, tens of thousands of acres had been cleared for pasture or plantation crops, ushering in an era that would ultimately result in the economic, racial, and cultural transformation of the Islands.

Although he would never join a church, Kamehameha III ultimately came to rely on the advice and the expertise of missionaries who accepted ministerial roles in the royal government. When kuhina nui Kīnaʻu died in 1839, Dr. Gerrit P. Judd quickly emerged as the most powerful of Kamehameha III's American ministers. Like William Richards, Hawaiʻi's first Minister of Public Instruction, Judd had arrived in Hawaiʻi as a missionary in 1828. Leaving the spiritual ministry for the political, Judd swore allegiance to the Hawaiian Kingdom and, with the support of Foreign Minister Robert Wyllie and Attorney General John Ricord, set out to frame a new government.

Far-reaching changes were accomplished in the years of Kamehameha III's reign by the king and his Western advisors. Hawaiʻi's first constitution was written in 1840, followed by a second in 1852. The legislature, providing a role for the aliʻi in the House of Nobles, was empowered to formulate laws to replace the kapu and royal edicts of the past. The right to vote was extended to Hawaiian males and select foreign residents. Finances were put in order and the treasury made solvent.

The Constitution of 1840 had made Hawaiʻi a kingdom under legislated laws, but it did not deal with the demands that permanent title to land should be granted to all. Until then, title to land had been vested with the king. His undivided ownership of the land was the last vestige of the feudal past. In 1848, under pressure to create legal standards for land ownership, the king undertook a division of the royal lands.

A thorough reorganization of the executive, legislative, judicial, and financial branches made Hawaiʻi's political institutions and laws conform to Western standards. *"It is indispensable to frame such a [law] code as those nations can understand and appreciate,"* Attorney General Ricord commented

Honolulu, 1837. Kamehameha III presides at an important assemblage gathered at Halekauwila Palace, his thatch residence. Included are chiefs and chiefesses, French and English naval officers, and advisors. At issue—the rights and practices of Catholic priests in Hawaiʻi. Lithograph by Louis-Jules Masselot.

American missionary William Alexander preaching on Kauaʻi, c. 1840. By then, Christianity had a strong foothold in Hawaiʻi, where it helped to fill the void left by collapse of the old gods in 1819. Steel engraving by Alfred Agate, artist for U.S. Exploring Expedition, 1840.

Born in 1803, missionary doctor Gerrit P. Judd joined Kamehameha III's government, which he served loyally for many years in a variety of roles that afforded him almost kingly authority during tumultuous years in which Hawaiʻi evolved into a Euro-style constitutional monarchy.

A thatch structure in sparsely populated Waikīkī serves as a place of quarantine for six passengers (including Paul Emmert, artist who painted this picture) arriving at Honolulu Harbor, February 10, 1853, when the city was in the throes of a smallpox epidemic. Of 6,405 cases, the death toll was 2,485. Smallpox, one of many introduced diseases that struck Native Hawaiians with epidemic force throughout the nineteenth century, reduced the population from approximately 150,000 to about 70,000 during Kamehameha III's reign.

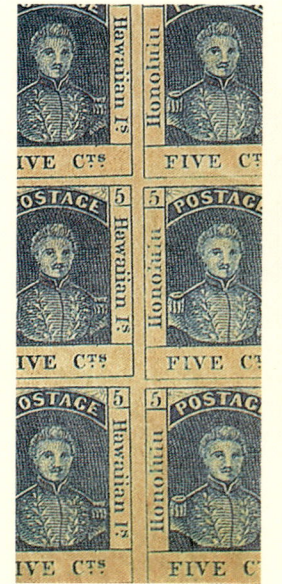

(Right) The Royal Seal, affixed to a land grant made possible by the land division of 1848, known as the Great Māhele. (Above right) A letter from Kamehameha III bears his personal royal stamp, one of many adaptations to Western culture introduced during his twenty-nine-and-a-half-year reign. (Above left) A block of postage stamps with the picture of Kamehameha III.

when explaining the need to revise laws involving land ownership as well. Under the guidance of Doctor Judd, a committee consisting of ali'i John Young II (also called Keoni Ana), J. Pi'ikoi, and Mataio Kekūanao'a had been organized to negotiate a māhele, or division, of feudal lands.

The first goal was to separate lands claimed by the king from those claimed by the konohiki, or royal landlords. Kamehameha III had made the first move, reserving one million acres as Crown Lands, claiming these as his personal property. Half of the remaining three million acres were surrendered by the king as Government Lands, "...to be managed, leased or sold, in accordance with the will of said Nobles and Representatives, for the benefit of the Hawaiian Government and to the dignity of the Hawaiian Crown."

Kauikeaouli / Kamehameha III | 26

The lands remaining were set aside to settle konohiki claims. From late January through early March 1848, the king negotiated 245 māhele, surrendering nearly 1.5, million acres in the process. The māhele itself acknowledged only a royal grant of title. Final approval came from the government's newly formed Land Commission. The commoners' turn would come in 1850, when they were given title to kuleana, land grants usually two or three acres in size, designed to make them freehold farmers. A lack of understanding regarding land ownership caused many kuleana to be lost by the Native Hawaiians. Within decades, title to thousands of acres meant to benefit Hawaiians had been returned to the government for lack of claimant or had fallen into non-Hawaiian hands.

Already debilitated by more than a decade of civil war, Kamehameha's consolidation of power was followed by a wide range of introduced diseases. With each passing decade the problem intensified. When Kamehameha III came to the throne, the Native population was 150,000, a fraction of the 300,000 or more Hawaiians estimated at the time of Cook's arrival in 1778. Kamehameha III experienced this tragedy firsthand. Neither of his two children by Queen Kalama survived infancy, mirroring the grim reality experienced by Hawaiian families of all classes.

Within another generation, the Hawaiian population would be halved yet again, dwindling to fewer than 30,000 by the end of Kalākaua's reign. Only with the intermarriage that followed the influx of Chinese, Japanese, Americans, and Europeans to the Islands later in the century, did the Hawaiian and part-Hawaiian population figures begin to increase.

Not only was the declining Hawaiian population a human tragedy, it was also a political disaster, depriving the crown of a solid constituency and emboldening nations with imperial ambitions to consider Hawai'i a candidate for colonization. In 1843, British commander George Paulet used the threat of force to coerce a demoralized Kamehameha III into surrendering his kingdom to British control. For more than five months, the Union Jack flew over Hawai'i.

(Left) Queen Kalama, wife of Kamehameha III, c.1850s. Although the royal couple had two sons (Keaweaweula I and Keaweaweula II, both died in infancy. The king adopted his half-sister Kīna'u's two sons, Alexander Liholiho and Lot Kapuāiwa, who became successfully Kamehameha IV and Kamehameha V. (Right) Albert Kūkā'ilimoku Kūnuiākea, son of Kamehameha III and ali'i Jane Lahilahi Young Ka'eo. His illegitimate birth separated him from the crown.

The French and Americans were quick to protest, prompting the British Foreign Office to reject Paulet's actions as "unwarranted" and without sanction. The British flag was lowered, with Hawaiian independence reaffirmed in a joint declaration issued by France and Great Britain.

The issue of Hawaiian independence had seemingly been settled in 1849, when, after a decade of negotiations, Britain, France, the U.S., and several smaller European nations signed a treaty to that effect. Many Americans, the largest, most vocal foreign community residing in the Islands, announced themselves for annexation. Kamehameha III was on the verge of seeking an American protectorate when Great Britain and France rallied to the king's support. While the monarchy was saved and the issue of annexation laid to rest for another generation, for Kauikeaouli there was to be no reprieve. By December 16, 1854, scarred by the battles fought for his people and the island kingdom he ruled, the forty-one-year old king, third of the Kamehamehas, was dead. ∎

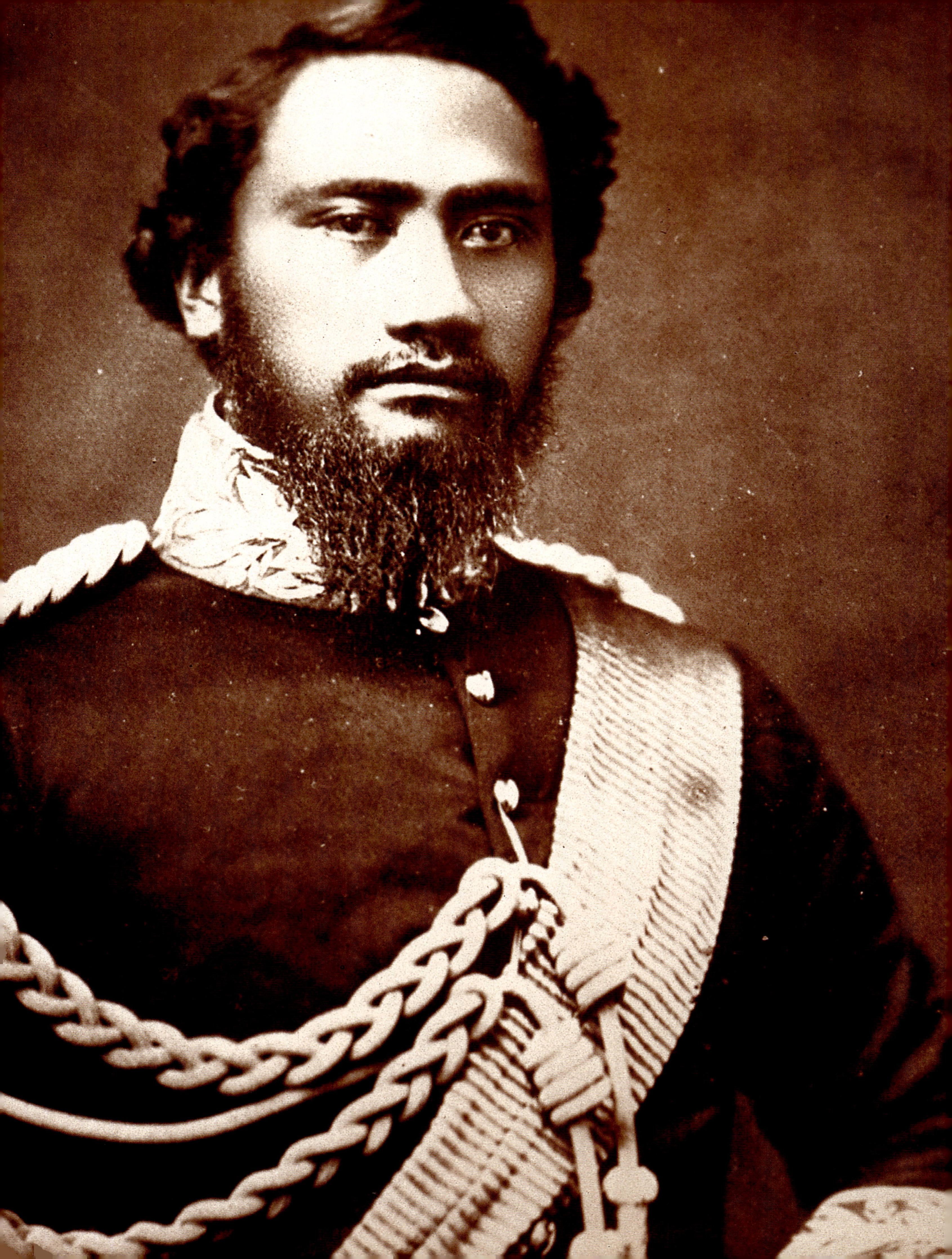

CHAPTER 6

ALEXANDER LIHOLIHO / KAMEHAMEHA IV
Turning to a New Generation (1854–1863)

Within an hour of the death of Kamehameha III, Mataio Kekūanaoʻa, governor of Oʻahu, proclaimed Alexander Liholiho, the late king's nephew and adopted son, as his successor. Kekūanaoʻa's haste established stability and unquestioned continuity to the monarchy. Kekūanaoʻa was also the new king's father. Alexander Liholiho's claim to the throne, however, came through his mother, Kīnaʻu, daughter of Kamehameha I and half-sister of the second and third Kamehamehas. In keeping with Hawaiian tradition, where hānai adoption played social and political roles, Alexander Liholiho had been adopted by Kamehameha III in 1853 to provide him with a direct-descent heir of high lineage.

Born on February 9, 1834, he was only twenty when he officially took claim to the throne in a ceremony at Kawaiahaʻo Church. Well-liked and respected for his wit, intelligence, and good looks, Alexander Liholiho had been raised to serve his people, starting with an education at the Chiefs' Children's School. In 1849, he and his older brother, Lot, accompanied envoy Judd on a tour of the U.S. and Europe designed to give them firsthand knowledge of the outside world.

Believing in the divine right of kings, Alexander Liholiho felt possessed of authority by virtue of his chiefly mana, although he would express it more in the style of a British royal than of a traditional Hawaiian chief. In ideas and tastes, the new king was decidedly an Anglophile. In addition to a strong distaste for the demanding and aggressive Americans who had settled in Hawaiʻi, the king had experienced American racial prejudice firsthand while visiting the United States. It had not left a favorable impression.

Robert Wyllie, the new king's Scots-born foreign minister, supported his king's pro-British feelings, understanding the political realities of the times. So did the queen, Emma Naea Rooke, in whose veins ran a mix of Hawaiian and English blood. Her grandfather was John Young, the British seaman who had been made an advisor by Kamehameha I. Childhood friends at the missionary-run Chiefs' Children's School in Honolulu, Emma and Alexander saw their friendship lead from love to courtship to marriage when, on June 19, 1856, Kamehameha IV made the twenty-year-old aliʻi his queen.

There were many reasons to favor the British, including their more sophisticated approach toward diplomacy and their respect for noble privilege. As both a man and a king, Alexander Liholiho found himself more in sympathy with British elitist beliefs than with the American missionaries. His affections for things British also had political ramifications.

Able men, both Native and foreign-born, assisted him in pursuit of royal priorities. Robert Wyllie was perhaps the most influential. As foreign minister and advisor to the king, he formulated and carried out foreign policy initiatives designed to secure international recognition of the sovereignty of the Hawaiian

A hand-tinted daguerreotype of Alexander Liholiho in the mid-1840s.

(Opposite) Kamehameha IV in full uniform. He was adopted by his uncle, Kamehameha III, who made him heir to the throne. Following extensive travel, he became far more Westernized in style and outlook than were his predecessors.

(Above) Memorabilia of Kamehameha IV—part of Bishop Museum's collections. (Bottom) In 1849, Gerrit P. Judd (standing) accompanied the princes Alexander Liholiho (right) and his brother Lot Kapu'aiwa to the United States and Europe to prepare them for future roles as kings. The trip left the impressionable Alexander Liholiho an Anglophile.

Kingdom, ending the king's seeking American annexation. Wyllie pursued treaties with the United States, Great Britain, and France that would jointly guarantee Hawai'i's independence. Kamehameha IV, however, understood America's commercial primacy in Hawai'i and accepted a proposed reciprocity treaty that would allow duty-free trade in sugar, textiles, and other commodities. An envoy was sent to Washington D.C., to meet with President Franklin Pierce. Months of discussions secured neither a joint guarantee nor the reciprocity treaty Kamehameha IV was after.

Even more disheartening was the failure to slow the continuing decline of the Hawaiian population. In a speech opening the legislature in 1855, the king dealt directly with the issue in no uncertain terms, calling "the decrease of our population...a subject, in comparison with which all others sink into insignificance."

He followed this observation with an appeal for funds to establish hospitals to serve the Hawaiian people. Despite royal pressure, it would take the government five years to open Queen's Hospital, named in honor of Queen Emma. Soon after, Dr. William Hillebrand would diagnose the first cases of leprosy (Hansen's disease), known then as ma'i pākē.

Within two years, a decision would be made for isolation of the afflicted, with hundreds sent into exile on the windswept Makanalua peninsula at the base of the towering cliffs along Moloka'i's rugged north coast.

With fewer than 70,000 Hawaiians left, Kamehameha IV realized that the kingdom might well need to import settlers to maintain a politically and commercially stable population base. The first contingent of foreign laborers, a shipload of 300 Chinese, arrived from Canton in 1852. In 1855, another 183 Chinese workers arrived. Isolated, exploited, and alien to both Hawaiian and Western experience, the Chinese failed to adapt to the plantation lifestyle.

Kamehameha IV did not have to look outside his own family for proof of the vulnerability of his people to disease and infertility. With heartfelt joy on May 20, 1858, his son Albert Edward Kauikeaouli Leiopapa, a Kamehameha, was born. The birth of Ka Haku o Hawai'i, the Prince of Hawai'i, as the infant was titled, confirmed the king's surrender to family life.

Minister Wyllie, who had already named his Kaua'i estate Princeville in honor of the child, and who planned to leave it to the Prince of Hawai'i in

A Kamehameha portrait, c. 1852. To secure succession, King Kamehameha III (center) and Queen Kalama (seated left), having lost their own two sons, adopt Kamehameha's nephew Alexander Liholiho (upper left) as son and name him heir to the throne. He becomes Kamehameha IV, 1854. His older brother Prince Lot (upper right) succeeds him, 1863, as Kamehameha V. Both Liholiho and Lot are sons of Kamehameha III's half-sister Kīna'u and Mataio Kekūanao'a. Their only daughter, Princess Victoria Kamāmalu, (seated right), is named heir apparent by Lot; but she dies before he does.

his will, wrote of the obvious pleasure the child brought the royal couple:

During the period that their Majesties condescended to be my guests [on Kaua'i], we were all quite charmed with the private life of the Royal pair...uniting in a just pride of and affection for their interesting and precocious son.

Kamehameha IV insured that the young Prince of Hawai'i was well-connected, naming him after the prince consort to Britain's Queen Victoria and choosing Albert and Victoria as godparents. The bond to the British royal family was further strengthened in 1860, when the king asked Victoria for her support in establishing an Anglican mission in Hawai'i, backing his request with a royal donation of land for a church and a $1,000 annual stipend for a qualified clergyman. The offer was accepted, and in August 1862, the Reverend Thomas Staley set sail from London, both to serve at the baptism of the Prince of Hawai'i and to establish an Anglican church in the Islands.

Auwe noho'i e! The ancient cry of grieving was soon heard again. On August 27, 1862, the Prince of Hawai'i, four years, three months, and seven days old, succumbed to a sudden illness. Both the royal family and the Hawaiian people mourned a lost prince whose death seemed to confirm their worst fears about their fate. "The death of no other person could have been so severe a blow to the king and his people," commented the *Pacific Commercial Advertiser* the day following his death.

Guilt over his son's death reenforced that of an earlier tragedy. In September 1859, while the royal family vacationed in Lāhainā, the king shot his friend and personal secretary, American-born Henry Neilson. The king had been agitated by rumors that Neilson had been romantically involved with Queen Emma. After his unwarranted outburst of jealousy, the remorseful king took responsibility for Neilson's welfare when he realized that the wounds placed his life in jeopardy. Two-and-a-half years later, several months before the death of the Prince of Hawai'i, Neilson died of complications resulting

Exterior view, fort at entrance to Honolulu Harbor, c. 1853. Rare surviving oil by Paul Emmert. Man addressing guards is O'ahu Governor Kekūanao'a whose house and office is long building with red roof.

31 | Alexander Liholiho / Kamehameha IV

A romantic Victorian collage of Hawaiian royals reveals newly wedded Emma Naea Rooke and Alexander Liholiho. Other members of the royal family are scattered about, including the king's father, Mataio Kekūanaoʻa (right of the king), his brother Lot (facing Kekūanaoʻa), and sister, Victoria Kamāmalu (far right). David Kalākaua and his wife Kapiʻolani are on the stairs.

Alexander Liholiho / Kamehameha IV

Posthumous oil on canvas by Enoch Wood Perry, Jr., c. 1864, of "Baby"—Albert Edward Kauikeaouli Leipopapa a Kamehameha—child of Kamehameha IV and Queen Emma. Known as the Prince of Hawai'i during his brief four-year life, he was heir to the throne and, tragically, the last child born to any Hawaiian monarch.

from the king's attack. The king may have felt partially responsible for the death of his son, having doused him with cold water to quiet a temper tantrum several days before he contracted the fever that would take his life. Self-imposed guilt began to assail the emotionally volatile king. The months that followed the deaths of Neilson and the Prince of Hawai'i drew the king closer to his Episcopal faith, even as his will to live was undermined by self-doubts and melancholia.

It is with emotions of deep sorrow that we record the death of Alexander Liholiho, who died Monday morning, November 30, at 15 minutes past 9 o'clock. He had been ill for some days, but no serious fears were entertained respecting him, until a few moments before he ceased to breathe. At the time of his death he was attended by Her Majesty the Queen, his venerable father, Mr. Wyllie, his physician and the household.

Kamehameha IV was dead at twenty-nine. ∎

Queen Emma (top) at twenty and King Kamehameha IV (bottom) at twenty-two, in a pair of unassuming studies in oil by English painter George Henry Burgess, 1856, the first year of their marriage.

33 | Alexander Liholiho / Kamehameha IV

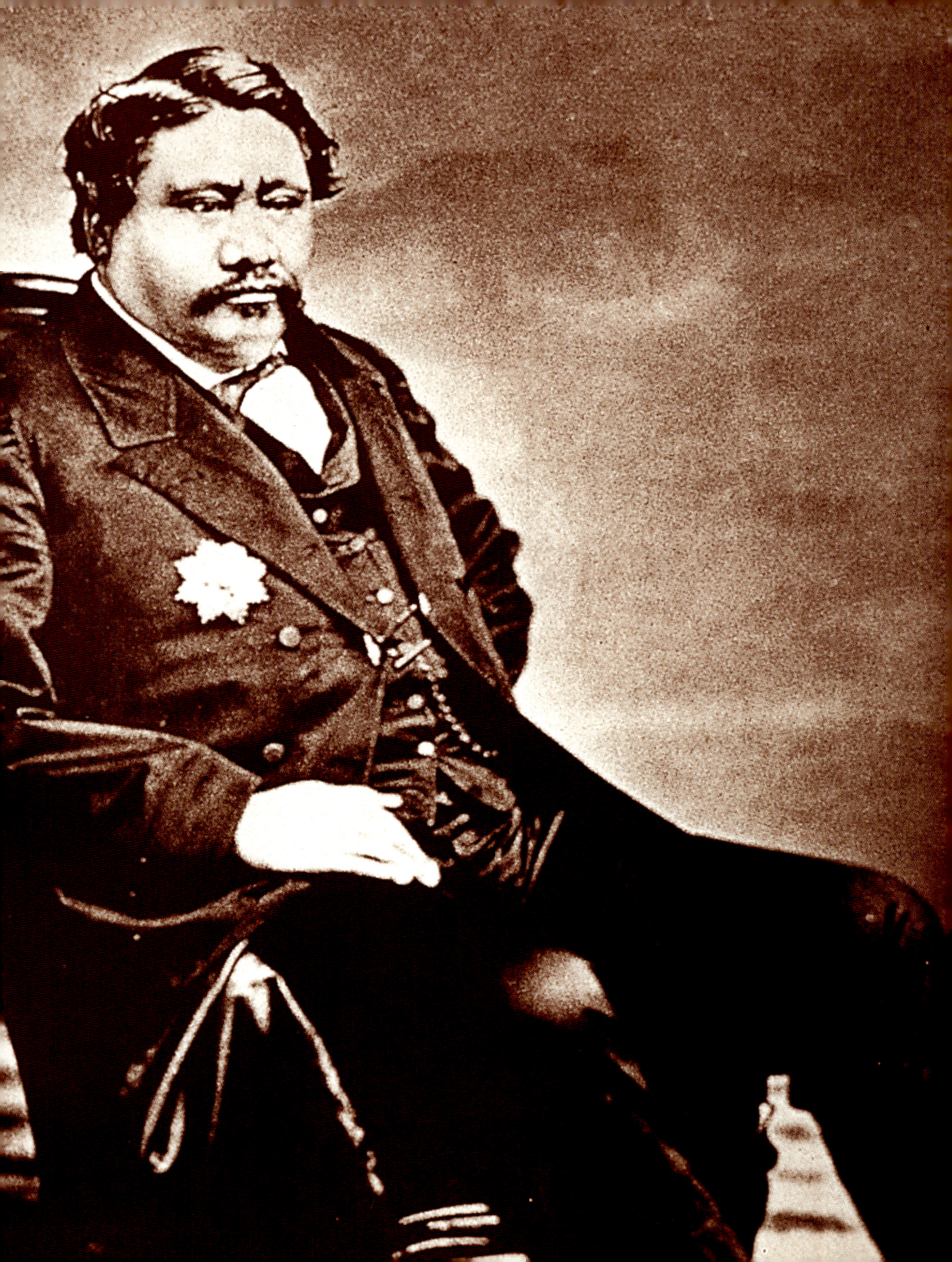

CHAPTER 7

★ LOT KAMEHAMEHA / KAMEHAMEHA V ★
Last of the Kamehameha Kings (1863–1872)

Prince Lot Kamehameha came to the throne by default. From childhood he had been deemed less capable than his younger brother, Alexander Liholiho, who had been chosen by their uncle, Kamehameha III, to carry on the dynasty. While none questioned the legitimacy of his mana or his right to the throne, there were many who questioned his ability to lead the nation. After he came to the throne as Kamehameha V, he proved his worth, projecting a steadiness, clarity, consistency, and focused calm.

Withdrawn and solemn, almost melancholy in temperament and appearance, he lacked the grace, charisma, and sophistication that made his brother well-loved. He, however, accepted the responsibilities of kingship without complaint or uncertainty. Engaged to his cousin Bernice Pauahi, Lot remained a bachelor when Pauahi fell in love and married Charles Reed Bishop in 1850. Lot's failure to marry or father an heir was the most serious omission of his reign.

Kamehameha V in full-dress uniform presents the king in westernized trappings of one who feels deeply his identity and inherent authority as a Hawaiian high chief. He was grandson of Kamehameha I and the elder brother of Kamehameha IV, who named Lot his successor. His accession as Kamehameha V was November 30, 1863.

To the surprise of many this underestimated prince proved an admirable monarch. His first act in reestablishing the authority of the crown was to refuse to take an oath to abide by the constitution that his brother and uncle had helped draft and implement. The constitution Lot rejected had been granted by Kamehameha III. Written by American-born Judge William L. Lee, the Constitution of 1852 forced the king to share power with a legislature made up of both Hawaiians and residents of foreign birth. While Kamehameha IV had pursued constitutional change that might restore royal authority, he was unsuccessful.

The new king quickly took the offensive. Using his cabinet as a forum, Lot debated ideas with men of varied backgrounds and opinions. Less of a romantic Anglophile than was his brother, he sought pragmatic solutions to Hawai'i's problems. While remaining a committed Christian, Kamehameha V distanced himself from the resident missionaries, whose approach and intentions he distrusted. Like his brother, Lot had developed an aver-

(Opposite) Remote, competent, and self-confident, Kamehameha V sought to reestablish a powerful role for the king by unilaterally proclaiming a new constitution.

Honolulu, 1867. It was midway through Kamehameha V's reign, and upper Fort Street was a quiet residential neighborhood. Watercolor over pencil by George Burgess.

Kamehameha V as a young man. Although, initially, there had been some doubt about his ability to rule, these concerns were quickly put to reset after he ascended the throne.

sion to their style and attitudes during his student years at mission-run schools. Five months after having ascended the throne, Lot announced his intent of securing a constitution that would increase the crown's power. Understanding the authority his presence commanded, the king set out on a six-week tour of his islands to muster support for constitutional change. The Hawaiians responded with the respect worthy of their new king's highborn rank.

Lot's concerns were paternal as well as political, for he saw the fate of his dynasty and the fate of his people as one and the same. Only a powerful Native Hawaiian king could maintain Hawai'i as a free and independent nation, and that meant a ruler with true authority and a constitution compatible with that goal. The constitution of 1864, while loosely based on that of 1852, did make changes that addressed the king's concerns. The position of kuhina nui, a now-ceremonial holdover from earlier days, was abolished, further consolidating royal power. The administrative authority of the king's appointed cabinet was also confirmed. Royal authority was further enhanced with the consolidation of legislative power in a single assembly that included both hereditary aliʻi and those elected to represent commoners and resident foreigners. In keeping with the king's wishes, property and literacy qualifications (for those born after 1840) were made preconditions for voting or serving in the legislature. Through force of will, political courage, and a clear sense of purpose, Kamehameha V was able to reassert monarchical power, but it would prove only a temporary reprieve, further alienating those who opposed subordination to royal authority.

Once constitutional issues were addressed, Kamehameha V was confronted by ongoing challenges. Most disheartening was the continuing decline of the Native Hawaiian population, which during Lot's reign fell to fewer than 60,000.

A thatch house, c. 1865, the window reflecting introduction of a Western architectural element to Hawaiian house design. At the time of this photograph, the Native Hawaiian population was in decline; and there was among this population a migration from rural areas to major towns.

In 1864, with the need for plantation labor as a catalyst, the government created the Board of Immigration. After a slow start, plantation agriculture had become a well-established component of the Hawaiian economy. From a diversity of crops introduced on the first plantation in Kōloa, Kauaʻi, in 1835, growers had come to focus primarily on sugar. By 1863, there were thirty-two sugar plantations in the kingdom.

The business of reprovisioning whaling ships, the mainstay of the Hawaiian economy since the 1830s, had peaked in the early 1850s. With the discovery of oil in Pennsylvania in 1859, whaling's days were numbered. Sugar, on the other hand, was a commodity with a future, thanks to events in the United States. The American Civil War created an instant American market for Hawaiʻi-grown sugar. By the time the Civil War ended in 1865, sugar had replaced whaling as the Hawaiian Kingdom's chief source of revenues. Sugar exports soared from 550,000 pounds in 1856 to twenty-three million pounds by 1873. While sugar created economic opportunities for many, it also made Hawaiʻi dependent on exports. America was the primary market and American growers played an increasingly significant and vocal role influencing the government's economic policies. What emerged was an uneasy alliance between resident American businessmen and the Hawaiian government.

The rapid growth of sugar determined Hawaiʻi's future. Labor intensive, it required more workers than the declining Hawaiian population could provide. The result was a tide of immigration that repopulated the mostly-deserted archipelago with non-Polynesian peoples. In September and October of 1865, 522 Chinese disembarked in Honolulu under contracts that earned them four dollars a month, plus housing, food, and medical care. The term of the contract was five years, after which they could return home. Three years later, 148 Japanese laborers arrived, signed to three-year contracts at similar wages. As

Mataio Kekūanaoʻa, a prominent chief and governor of Oʻahu, with his daughter Victoria Kamāmalu. Kekūanaoʻa was also father to Kamāmalu's brothers Alexander Liholiho (Kamehameha IV) and Lot Kapuaiwa (Kamehameha V).

Lot Kamehameha / Kamehameha V I

with the contract laborers who followed them, many would remain in the islands by extending their contracts or establishing themselves as skilled workers and businessmen when their contracts had expired. Kamehameha V was soon aware of the difficulties of absorbing culturally and racially different peoples.

Although the king was not in the best of health, there was no particular cause for alarm when he fell ill as preparations were being made for his forty-second birthday. It became obvious, however, that his condition was rapidly deteriorating. All efforts focused on getting him to name a successor. Since his sister, Victoria Kamāmalu, had died in 1866, the kingdom had been without a designated heir. Not until he lay on his deathbed several days later did the king finally name his cousin, Bernice Pauahi, who quickly refused. For the stubborn king, never one to readily compromise, the choice had been made. Pauahi remained steadfast in her refusal. On the night of December 11, 1872, the king's forty-second birthday, little more than eighty years after the first Kamehameha had made Hawai'i a united kingdom, the last of the Kamehameha kings surrendered his dynasty to history. ∎

Whaling, the mainstay of the Hawaiian economy for forty years, began a precipitous decline during Kamehameha V's reign. Sugar, on the other hand, was in the midst of a boom when this picture of the Hāna Plantation on Maui was taken in the late 1800s.

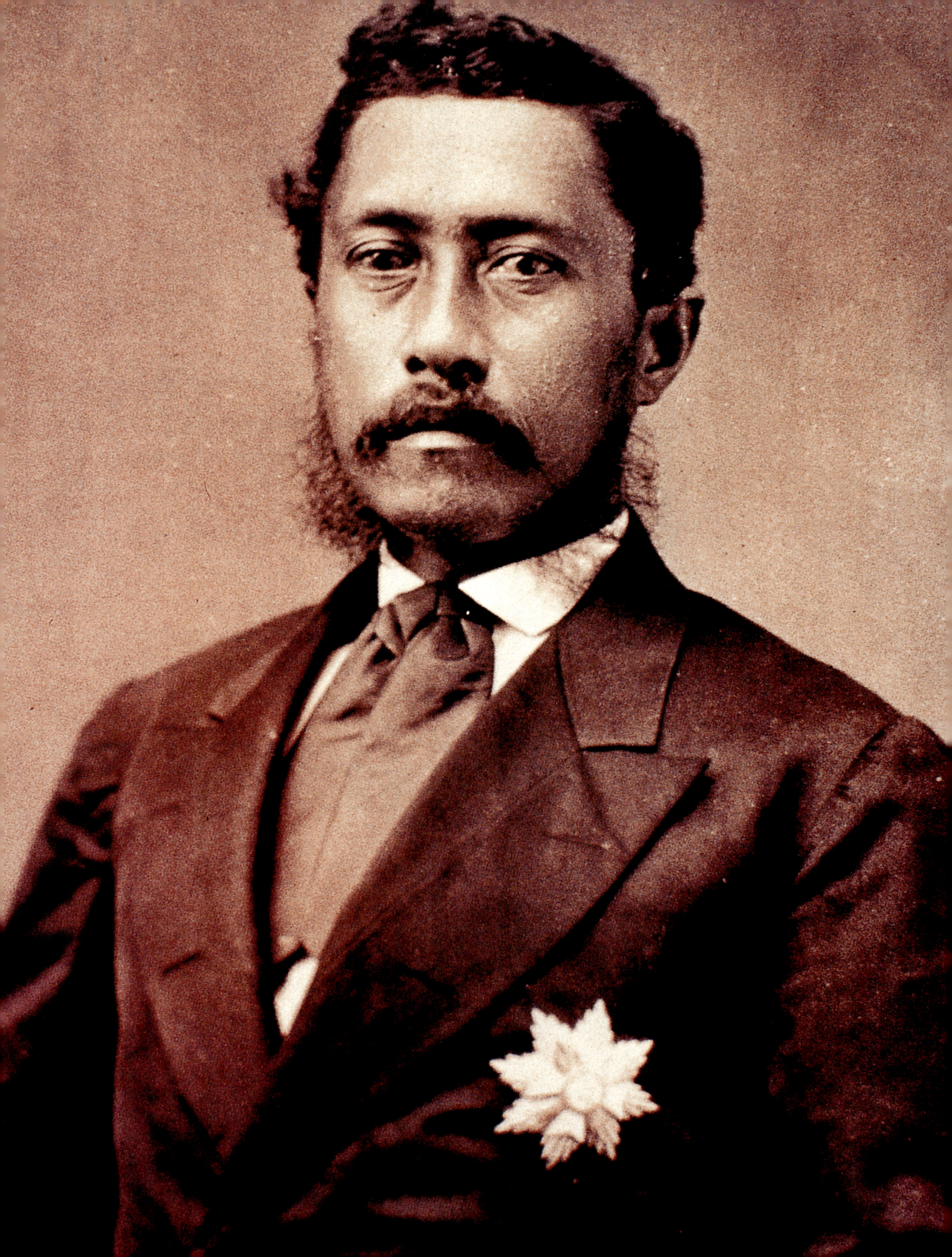

CHAPTER 8

WILLIAM CHARLES LUNALILO
False Start for a New Dynasty (1873–1874)

A mournful cry announced the passing of Kamehameha V on December 11, 1872, his forty-second birthday. Of immediate concern was the lack of an heir, Kamehameha's deathbed request to his cousin Bernice Pauahi Bishop having been rejected. Elections were immediately scheduled to provide Hawai'i with a new ruler. The choices narrowed down to the princes David Kalākaua and William Charles Lunalilo.

Lunalilo was considered a bon vivant by many, self-indulgent and far too fond of drink. However, the legitimacy of his mana consecrated his rule in the eyes of the Hawaiian people. Kamehameha V made an accurate appraisal of the situation shortly before he died:

My cousin William, however unworthy, still to the Natives, represents the ancient line of Kings, and as such would command their suffrages.

Lunalilo's affable personality and democratic leanings appealed to many Hawaiians as well as to the majority of resident foreigners, who hoped he would prove more open to compromise than had his predecessor. A plebiscite was held on January 1, 1873. Lunalilo had received near universal approval. The outcome was confirmed by the legislature one week later. The Citizen King, as Lunalilo came to be called, now sat on the Hawaiian throne. The following day, barefoot and reverent, seeking to set a new royal style and thereby inspire his people, Lunalilo walked to Kawaiaha'o Church to take the oath of office. There was optimism in the air as thousands cheered him.

Most of Lunalilo's short reign was consumed with two issues that would lead to an anti-foreign backlash. One involved securing the long-desired reciprocity treaty to allow Hawaiian sugar to enter the United States duty-free. The other involved American interest in securing rights to the deep-water anchorage at Pearl Harbor for a naval and commercial port. The two issues were closely linked. By

Prince William Lunalilo, 1847, at the age of twelve. Portrait suggesting a quiet demeanor is said to have been uncharacteristic of the outgoing "Prince Bill." Oil on canvas by Joel Blakeslee Knapp.

(Opposite) Called the Citizen King for his unassuming ways, William Charles Lunalilo kept pomp and circumstance to a minimum. On his chest, the Order of Kamehameha.

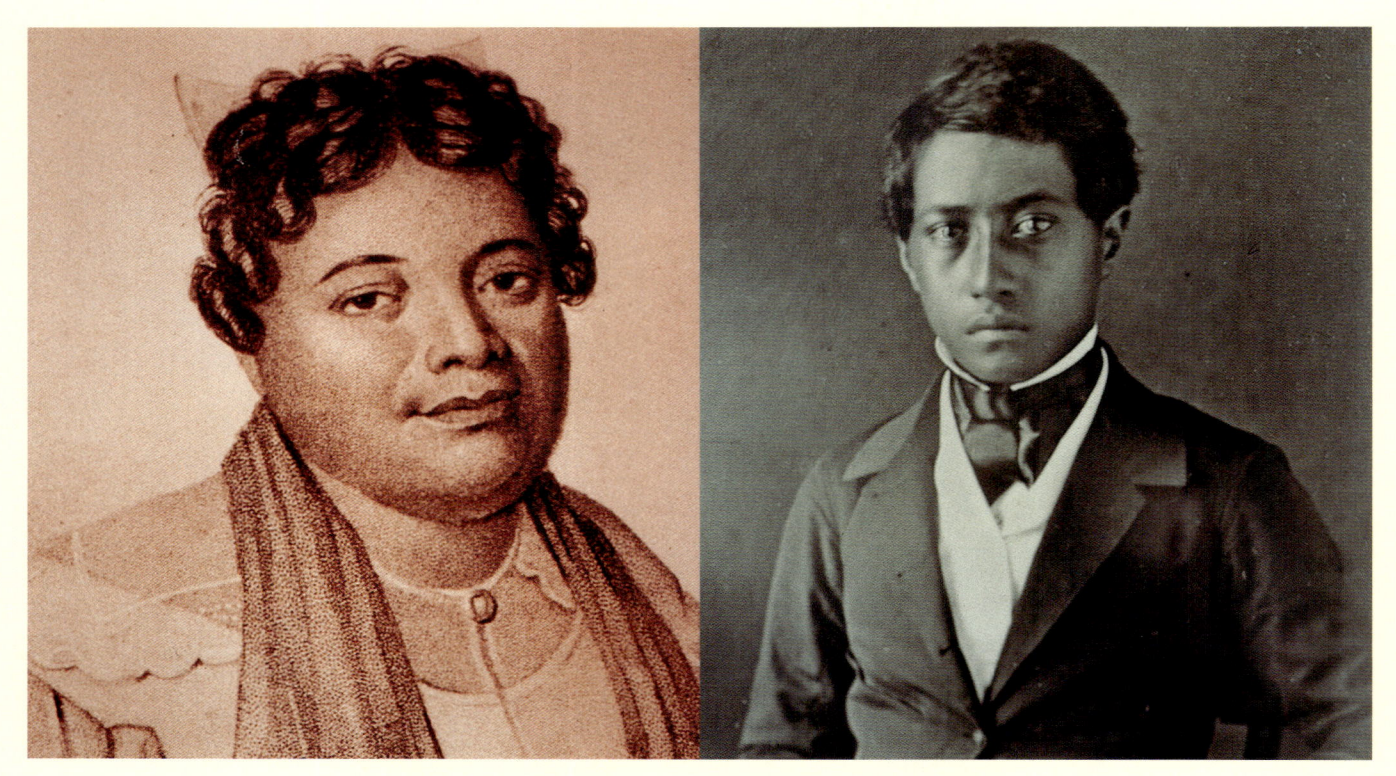

(Left) Lunalilo's mother, Chiefess Miriam Kekāuluohi, became Hawai'i's third kuhina nui (premier, co-ruler), 1839, serving with Kamehameha III under the title of Ka'ahumanu III until her death, 1845. (Right) A daguerreotype of Lunalilo as a young man.

William Charles Lunalilo (seated, second from left) and David Kalākaua (seated, extreme right), c. 1872, while both were still future kings. Others (left to right): Major Moehonua; Dave McKinley (possibly); J.J. Kekoulahao; California writer Charles W. Stoddard; Fred K. Beckley.

William Charles Lunalilo

February 1873, American use of Pearl Harbor was being openly considered in exchange for the long-desired reciprocity treaty. However, public opposition to such a leasing of the ʻāina quelled any serious negotiation with Washington.

In September, the Royal Household Troops rebelled against the rigid discipline of foreign-born drillmaster Joseph Jajczay. Lunalilo, though suffering from illness, convinced his royal guards to give up their brief mutiny and return to their barracks in peace. After mediating that crisis, the matter of the king's deteriorating health became of concern, his well-being compromised by a lifetime of indulgence and dissipation. Tuberculosis set in, complicated by alcoholism. Despite such concerns, Lunalilo could not be induced to name a successor.

On February 3, 1874, one year and twenty-five days after his reign had begun, the Lunalilo dynasty drew to a close. Kealiʻi lokomaikaʻi, "the kind chief" as his people lovingly called him, had departed. His father, the aging Charles Kanaʻina, supervised the construction of a Victorian-style mausoleum adjacent to Kawaiahaʻo Church. There, far from the aliʻi who preceded and followed him on Hawaiʻi's throne, William Charles Lunalilo, "highest of the highborn," was laid to rest. ∎

Lunalilo (right) as a young man with his father, Charles Kanaʻina. Cousin to the Kamehamehas, Lunalilo resented what he considered their rude treatment of his mother, Chiefess Kekauluohi.

43 | William Charles Lunalilo

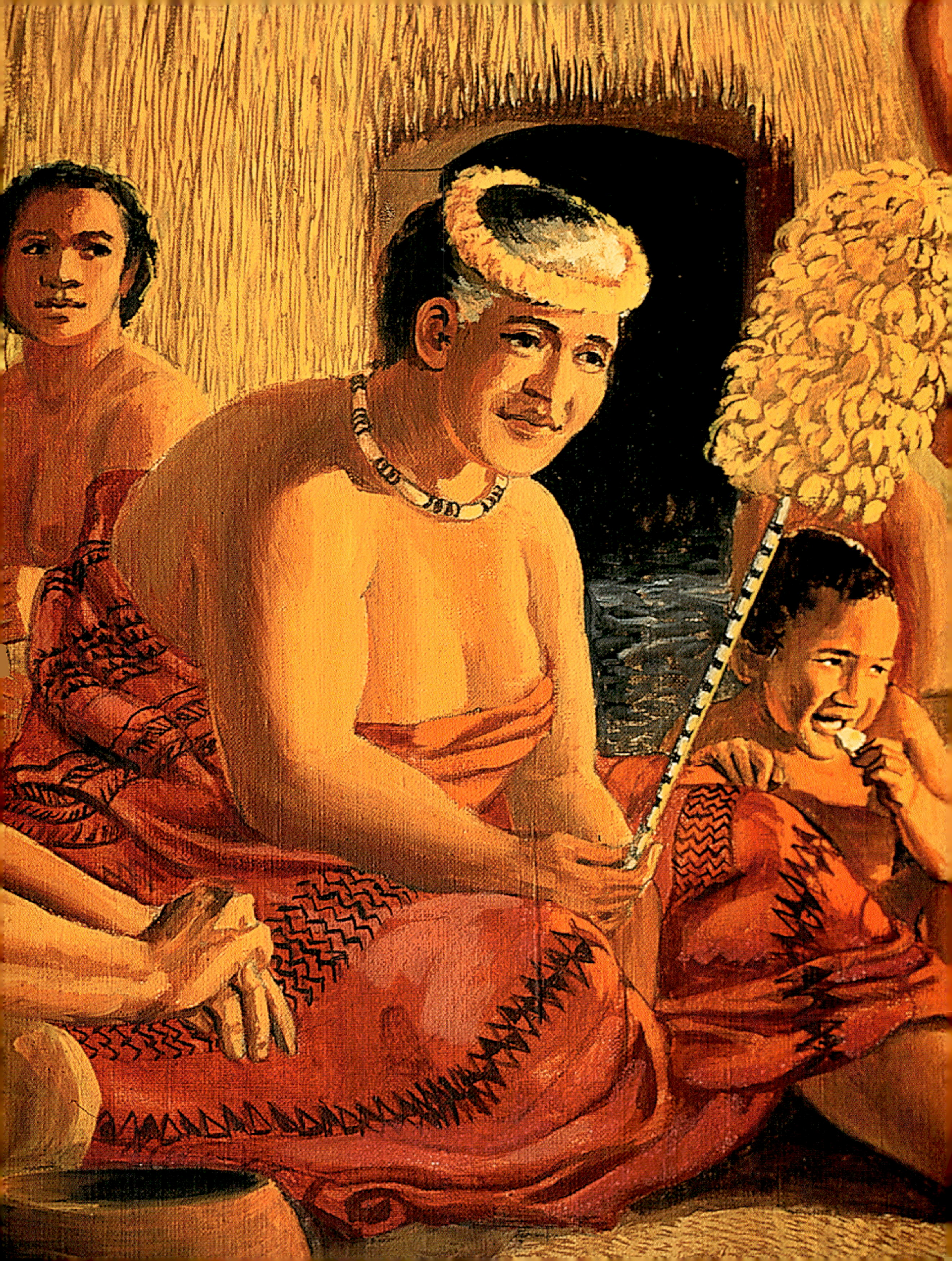

CHAPTER 9

THE ROYAL WOMEN

Powerful Wāhine are a Part of Hawaiian History

While all but one of Hawai'i's ruling monarchs were men, ali'i women exerted very real political and spiritual influence. In many generations, ali'i women genealogically outranked ali'i men. The kapu system recognized their high status, and the ruling chiefs were very careful to select women of the highest mana for the children they might bear. Those who were also intelligent, motivated, charismatic, and aggressive might actually rule, as did Ka'ahumanu and Kīna'u during the reigns of the second and third Kamehameha kings. Or they might exert influence behind the scenes, as did Keōpūolani, sacred wife of Kamehameha and mother of these same two kings. Each generation undoubtedly produced women of high status, strong will, authority, and competence—women enriched and ennobled by high birth, intrigued by the uses of power, and beneficiaries of exalted mana and great wealth. By the nineteenth century, almost all of the private wealth of the royal, era was concentrated in the estates of a few ali'i women. The nineteenth-century female ali'i provide an insight into the role highborn women played throughout the long span of Hawai'i's Polynesian history.

Early Hawaiian historian S. M. Kamakau considered Ka'ahumanu "the most beautiful woman in Hawai'i…six feet tall…without blemish." Twenty-first century artist Herb Kane depicts her smiling, with a feather lei on her head. The lei and the hand kahili symbolize her chiefly rank.

Artist Herb Kane depicts Kapi'olani (1781–1841), as she challenges volcano goddess Pele, 1824. The strong-willed Kapi'olani was married to national orator Nāihe; she herself was of high chiefly lineage, the daughter of Keawema'uhili, a kapu chief, and of Kekikipa'a, daughter of Kame'eiamoku. An early convert to Christianity, she led a march from Kona to the edge of Kīlauea Volcano fire pit, where she defied the goddess Pele by breaking the tabu and proclaiming the might of Jehovah. Her party withdrew without being consumed by an enraged deity, and the Protestant mission at Hilo gained numerous converts therefrom. The drama of Kapi'olani's expression of faith inspired the writing of Alfred, Lord Tennyson's poem, "Kapiolani."

KA'AHUMANU (c. 1768–1832)

Ka'ahumanu was born in a cave fronting the sea in Hāna, Maui, about 1768. Her warrior father, Ke'eaumoku, a high chief from Kona, had been one of the most prominent supporters of Kamehameha in the civil wars that led to the unification of the islands. It was Ke'eaumoku who had killed the half-brothers Kīwala'ō and Keōua, Kamehameha's rivals for supremacy on the island of Hawai'i in the 1780s. Named as administrator of the island in appreciation of his loyalty, Ke'eaumoku succumbed to bubonic plague while visiting O'ahu in 1804.

Ka'ahumanu's mother, Nāmāhana, was also of high ali'i status amongst Maui's chiefly families. Before marrying Ke'eaumoku, she had been one of Kamehameha's first wives. Twenty years later, Ka'ahumanu would become Kamehameha's wife and lovemate. A contemporary picture of Ka'ahumanu, painted by Louis Choris in 1816 when she was already in her forties, shows a woman of strength and beauty. Six-feet tall and weighing more than 200 pounds, she was a match for Kamehameha in scale, intelligence and self-confidence.

A portrait of Kaʻahumanu in her late forties, by Louis Choris, 1816.

When Kamehameha died in 1819, Kaʻahumanu claimed that he had empowered her to serve as kuhina nui, or advisor and regent, for his son Liholiho who was considered unprepared for the responsibilities of leadership. When none challenged her claim, Kaʻahumanu allied herself with Keōpūolani, mother of the Kamehameha princes, and quickly set out to challenge the established order. The opportunity came within months of Kamehameha's death, when the two aliʻi women broke the ʻai kapu, the sacred eating prohibition against men and women eating together. Publicly feasting with Keōpūolani and Liholiho's brother, the child-prince Kauikeaouli, was a first proof that without Kamehameha's moral authority the old order would collapse from within even before it would be challenged by threats from outside. As kuhina nui, Kaʻahumanu influenced Kamehameha II during the four years of his reign, although the willful young king was not always amenable to her suggestions. At times she took the initiative, effectively pursuing power, neutralizing opposition both real and potential. In 1821 she married both Kaumualiʻi, vassal king of Kauaʻi, and his handsome twenty-three-year-old son, Kealiʻahonui, when Liholiho brought them back to Oʻahu as royal prisoners. Within three years, Kaumualiʻi was dead, poisoned, his son claimed, in an effort to eliminate potential opposition to the rule of the Kamehamehas.

In November 1823, Kaʻahumanu secured effective control of the kingdom when Liholiho departed Honolulu for London. Having asserted her influence during the reign of the first Kamehameha, Kaʻahumanu did not hesitate to rule authoritatively as regent for Kamehameha II. Six months after his departure, Kaʻahumanu proclaimed a new code of civil laws designed to replace the kapu she had effectively helped eliminate. Based on missionary teaching, these new laws forbade a number of Ten Commandment sins, outlawing murder, theft, fighting, and breaking the Sabbath in an effort to restrain social chaos caused by the foreign seamen hell-bent on pleasure and drink.

In 1825, Kaʻahumanu's authority as kuhina nui was further enhanced when eleven-year-old Kauikeaouli succeeded Liholiho as Kamehameha III following his brother's death in London. With a minor on the throne, Kaʻahumanu was more readily accepted as regent than she had been when Kamehameha II was king. There was still opposition to her rule among the remaining traditionalist chiefs and kāhuna, who resented her acceptance of foreign values and her heavy-handed use of royal authority.

Instrumental in precipitating the collapse of the old order, Kaʻahumanu was not quick to convert to the new religion. Having granted a year's right of residence to the New England missionaries who had arrived in 1820, she initially watched from a distance for several years. In 1825, having been taught to read, write, and seek the salvation the missionaries preached, Kaʻahumanu converted to Christianity.

By 1827, she had become a vocal supporter of Protestant missionaries, opposing the efforts of French Catholic priests wanting to settle in Hawaiʻi whom she expelled. The French government viewed this as an insufferable insult and responded with angry demands that were accepted under threat of war. It was a prelude to problems that would confront the monarchy for the remainder of its existence. When Kaʻahumanu died on June 5, 1832, the dynasty her husband had founded was being undermined by the increasing numbers of foreigners settling in the kingdom. Though possessed of an iron will and an openness to change, she left behind a kingdom unprepared for changes already under way.

KEŌPŪOLANI (c. 1775–1823)

Kamehameha the Great was more than twenty years old when the highborn aliʻi Keōpūolani, daughter of his first cousin Kīwalaʻō, who had lost his life fighting in 1782, was born. Her mother, Kekuʻiapoiwanui Liliha, was a half-sister of Kīwalaʻō, a union that made Keōpūolani's mana sacred, her status enhanced by links to the ruling chiefs of Maui. Keōpūolani's grandmother, the chiefess Kalola, had made a deathbed request to Kamehameha to take charge of both the widowed Liliha and her infant daughter. Kamehameha made Liliha his wife and, many years later, also married Keōpūolani. It was Keōpūolani's exalted mana that motivated Kamehameha, for through her his children would be of the highest aliʻi rank. Also by fathering children with Kīwalaʻō's daughter, the rift between the two branches of the ancient ruling House of Keawe would be healed. Her mana ensured the Kamehameha dynasty's claim to the throne.

For Keōpūolani, being of high birth meant a life proscribed by numerous kapu. Her mana was such that, should a commoner see her or accidentally cast a shadow on her or her possessions, death was the possible outcome. It was said that she traveled only at night, hidden from public view for fear of risking the lives of those of lower rank. Even the esteemed Kamehameha was her inferior in terms of mana, and he had to prostrate himself when in her presence. Part of Keōpūolani's motivation in supporting the overthrow of the old order in 1819 may have been the result of the inhibiting restraints placed on her by kapu. Joining Kaʻahumanu, she first broke the dining kapu by eating with her younger son, Kauikeaouli, at a public lūʻau. Some months later her older son, ruling as Kamehameha II, followed her lead, publicly feasting with her and Kaʻahumanu, and calling for an end to the power of the priests and the kapu. In 1823, just before her death, Keōpūolani became one of the first converts of the Protestant missionaries. Symbol of the old order yet committed to change, she died before the consequences of her actions could be evaluated.

LILIHA (c. 1796–1842)

The daughter of Hoapili Kāne, companion-in-arms to Kamehameha I and subsequently governor of Maui, Liliha was also the granddaughter of the Maui chiefess Kalola. She was still an impetuous teenager when she married high chief Boki, a friend and adventuring companion to the young Kamehameha II. A couple of exotic beauty, Boki and Liliha accompanied Kamehameha II and Queen Kalama to London.

With the death of Kamehameha II, Boki and Liliha found themselves in opposition to Kaʻahumanu's emerging power. Boki used his position as governor of Oʻahu to let Kaʻahumanu's new laws of temperance and restraint be breached, actually selling alcohol in open violation. Pressured by older chiefs to modify his behavior and fearful of retribution, Boki departed Hawaiʻi in December 1829, for the New Hebrides Islands, in search of a new source of sandalwood, now that Hawaiʻi's forests had been depleted of this fragrant resource. The venture was in partnership with the king, as both Boki and Kamehameha III hoped to reap large profits from the enterprise. The government provided two refitted brigs, the *Kamehameha* and the *Becket*. The ships, with a crew of 400, made it safely to Fiji. Several weeks later, however, the *Kamehameha* was lost at sea with Boki aboard.

Liliha had stayed behind, serving as governor of Oʻahu in Boki's stead. She continued his revenue-generating noncompliance with the law, reaching a point just short of rebellion in 1831, when she prepared to resist a royal decree removing her from the governor's position. She was finally dissuaded from resistance by her father, Hoapili, governor of Maui, who sailed to

Although no contemporaneous images of Keōpūolani are known to have survived, this lithograph details the "lamentations on the Death of Queen Keōpūolani in 1823." Despite the traditional mourning ritual that accompanied the death of this sacred aliʻi, the Western clothes of the mourners indicate societal change.

The Royal Women

Chiefess Liliha in aliʻi attire. Liliha married Chief Boki when she was still in her teens. They both accompanied Kamehameha II and Queen Kamāmalu to England, where both Hawaiian monarchs died of measles. Back in Honolulu, where the young Kauikeaouli ascended the throne as Kamehameha III, Liliha's influence on the new king was cause for concern among the more conservative chiefs. Portrait by John Hayter.

Honolulu from Lāhainā to talk with his headstrong daughter. Forced to surrender the governorship to Kaʻahumanu, who quickly passed the position on to her brother, Kuakini, Liliha retired to Lāhainā.

She spent the last eight years of her life in Maui, opposing the missionaries. It was not a popular position to take, for with each passing year the number of converts grew. Later, Kamehameha III, in an effort to free himself of missionary influence, tried to substitute Liliha for Kīnaʻu as kuhina nui. The move, however, was rejected by the Council of Chiefs, and Liliha became an increasingly peripheral figure. In 1839, when most of the holdout aliʻi finally accepted Christianity, Liliha herself became a convert. Within three years Liliha was dead.

NĀHIʻENAʻENA (c. 1815–1836)

Youngest of the three children of Kamehameha and Keōpūolani, Nāhiʻenaʻena was educated by the American missionaries. Pampered and indulged as a privileged aliʻi on the one hand, she was judged harshly by her missionary teachers, one of many aliʻi to suffer the consequences of contact with the ideals and morality of the Christian world. In 1824, after Kamehameha II set sail for England, Nāhiʻenaʻena, a confused and willful child of nine, temporarily rejected missionary teachings in favor of the gods of old Hawaiʻi. Her commitment, however, came at a time when the aliʻi and priests were too disorganized and demoralized to mount a sustained effort on behalf of the gods who were being discredited. She would eventually recommit to Christian belief. For most of her short life, she was emotionally, morally,

The nīʻaupiʻo Princess Nāhiʻenaʻena (1816-1836) at the age of nine. The daughter of Kamehameha I and Keopuolani, she was sister to both Kamehameha II and Kamehameha III. Portrait by Robert Dampier on the H.M.S. *Blonde* with George, Lord Byron, 1825.

The Royal Women

and spiritually at odds with herself, uncertain in her beliefs and loyalties. The inner conflict culminated over the issue of marrying Kamehameha III. By the standards of the past, such a bonding between sister and brother was considered sacred, producing offspring of the highest aliʻi status. While many of the older chiefs anticipated such a union as a means of further strengthening the royal bloodline, missionary opposition, manifest in the opposition of converts like Kīnaʻu, derailed a possible union. What had previously been sacred was now a mortal sin. She married high chief Leleiōhoku in 1835 and settled in Lāhainā where the royal court had temporarily transferred. Nāhiʻenaʻena continued to suffer the inner conflict of one caught between two worlds. She died within a year, possibly of a broken spirit, her will to live compromised. She was a tragic symbol of a spiritual malaise that affected many of her generation.

KĪNAʻU (c. 1805–1839)

Daughter of Kamehameha and Kalākua, niece of Kaʻahumanu, Kīnaʻu assumed the role of kuhina nui after Kaʻahumanu's death in 1832. In two separate proclamations addressed primarily to the aliʻi, Kamehameha III and his half-sister announced their intentions at cooperative rule in an effort to assure the continuity of the government at a time of transition. Their dual pronouncement, however, only confused the issue of the true extent of Kīnaʻu's authority. The young king clearly stated his position when naming her kuhina nui:

I am superior and my mother [meaning Kīnaʻu, actually his half-sister] *subordinate. She is my chief Agent…We two who have been too young and unacquainted with the actual transaction of business, now for the first time undertake to distinctly regulate our kingdom.*

Kīnaʻu's pronouncement acknowledged the king, but emphasized her authority as well:

The office which my mother [meaning Kaʻahumanu, actually her aunt] *held until her departure is now mine. All her active duties and authority are committed to me. The tabus of the king, and the law of God, are with me, and also the laws of the King. My appointment as chief agent is of long standing, even from our father* [Kamehameha]…

Committed to enforcing the missionary-inspired laws instituted by Kaʻahumanu, Kīnaʻu soon found herself opposed by Kamehameha III, a still-unsettled, self-indulgent eighteen-year-old. Like his sister Nāhiʻenaʻena, he was caught between a past no longer intact and a future as yet undefined. Kīnaʻu's conflict with Kamehameha III brought an unexpected result when in 1834 the young king unilaterally abrogated most of Kaʻahumanu's Old Testament laws. In alliance with the tradition-minded older chiefs, Kīnaʻu sought to stabilize a society already adrift. Still unready for the rigors of kingship, Kamehameha III yielded to her efforts in 1835, surrendering to Kīnaʻu's authority. For the remaining four years of her life, she effectively controlled the royal government, extending her influence into the next generation when the childless Kamehameha III adopted her sons, Lot and Alexander Liholiho, naming the latter heir-presumptive to the throne. Lot would follow Alexander Liholiho as Kamehameha V. The four years she ruled as kuhina nui were not without periods of despair for the sensitive Kīnaʻu. Confiding in missionary wife Mrs. Gerrit Judd, she revealed a deep-rooted anxiety that afflicted many Hawaiians as the nineteenth century unfolded:

The Chiefess Kīnaʻu was one of the first converts to Christianity, is seen here with attendants, after a Sunday morning at Kawaiahaʻo Church. Lithograph by Louis-Jules Masselot, artist aboard *La Venus*, with Du Petit-Thouars, 1837.

49 | The Royal Women

I am in straits and heavy-hearted...I am quite discouraged, and cannot bear this burden any longer. I wish to throw away my rank, and title, and responsibility [and] bring my family here [to the Judd home] *or...take our families and go to America.*

It is impossible to determine what might have happened had Kīna'u lived longer. Already in 1837 she had been warned that the autocratic power of the king and his kuhina nui was no longer valid, and a constitutional monarchy was becoming a necessity. This would come in 1840, by authority of Kamehameha III. By then, Kīna'u would have been dead for more than a year, the kingdom she had worked to preserve surrendered to changes Hawai'i's monarchy could no longer resist.

RUTH KE'ELIKŌLANI (c. 1826–1883)

None of the royal women were as enigmatic as Ruth Ke'elikōlani. More than six feet tall and weighing over 400 pounds, she combined the authority of imposing dimensions, with a lineage of high ali'i rank and an imperial personality that intimidated all but the handful she deemed worthy of trust and aloha. Dressed in Victorian finery and builder of an extravagant Victorian mansion, she remained Hawaiian in language, habits, temperament, and belief.

Born in the royal compound of Pohukaina, Honolulu, in 1826, Ruth was the great-granddaughter of Kamehameha I by his granddaughter, Pauahi, and Mataio Kekūanao'a. When her mother died in childbirth, the newborn infant was placed under the care of Ka'ahumanu, who provided a traditional ali'i role model that would influence her entire life. Unfortunately, Ka'ahumanu died when Ruth was only six. Later, when her father, Mataio Kekūanao'a, married Kīna'u, Ruth was accepted as a part of their family, raised as sister to their four children, including the future kings Alexander Liholiho and Lot Kapu'aiwa. Ruth was only fifteen when she was married for the first time, to Leleiōhoku, son of Kamehameha's chief advisor Kalanimōkū.

William Pitt Kīna'u (also known as John Pitt Kīna'u), Ruth's second child by Leleiōhoku, died in 1859, at age seventeen.

Princess Ruth Ke'elikōlani (1826-1883), attended by Sam Parker (left) and John A. Cummins, c. 1877. Each man wears a feathered cap, symbol of chiefly blood; and each holds a kāhili over Ruth, symbol of her exalted rank. Both men were socially prominent in royal circles of the period.

The Royal Women | 50

The first of her two children died in infancy when Ruth was only sixteen. Six years later, in 1848, Ruth lost her husband to a measles epidemic, when he was only twenty-seven and she was twenty-two. Her second son, William Pitt Kīnaʻu, died just short of his seventeenth birthday, when Ruth was only thirty-three. In 1856, Ruth married the strong-willed part-Hawaiian Isaac Young Davis, grandson and namesake of the Welsh mate captured and recruited as an advisor to Kamehameha I. The marriage was stormy and, after little more than a year, Ruth left, but not before giving birth to a son. In keeping with Hawaiian tradition, Ruth offered the child in hānai, or adoption, to Bernice Pauahi. The child died six months later.

With hope that defied fate, Ruth next adopted the younger son of Kapaʻakea and Keohokālole. Renaming him Leleiōhoku in honor of her long-dead husband, she made him beneficiary to her inherited wealth of the Kamehamehas. Handsome and cultured, Leleiōhoku would also be named heir-apparent to the Hawaiian throne when his older brother, David Kalākaua, was elected king in 1814. Had he come to the throne, the immense land wealth of the Kamehamehas would have been reconciled with a ruling king, with fiscal and spiritual implications for the monarchy and Hawaiian independence. Once again death intervened. On April 9, 1877, Leleiōhoku died of pneumonia while at ʻIolani Palace.

In August 9, 1881, lava had been flowing down the flanks of Mauna Loa for more than six months and a river of molten rock sixty miles long was approaching Hilo. Prayers to the Christian god had failed to stop the flow. Ruth, heir to ancient beliefs and confident that her mana remained strong, decided to play an intermediary's role, traveling by steamer from Oʻahu to the island of Hawaiʻi. Making her way up-country, accompanied by a small retinue, she stood poised in imposing silhouette against a night sky lit by the lava's red-orange glow. With prayers, chants, and offerings, she confronted Pele, speaking to the goddess both as supplicant and aliʻi. Telling her retainers to prepare a bed for her not far from the front of the flow, she spent the night alone in Pele's fiery domain. A letter from one of her party set the scene:

> *Early the next morning all of us went to the lava flow and we couldn't believe our eyes. The flow had stopped right there. Suddenly our feeling toward the Princess changed. We were one and all awed. When the Princess returned to Honolulu, a tremendous crowd greeted her at the dock. The streets were jammed. It didn't take long for the story to flash around the islands.*

Her mana and prestige enhanced, Ruth committed her money and time to building a Victorian mansion in the style and scale of the new ʻIolani Palace, just completed by Kalākaua. The house, called Keōuahale, was completed in 1883, with Ruth spending several nights there following a grand opening that was a gala social event. Within days of the festivities she became ill and decided that it was time to return to the island of Hawaiʻi. Once there, she took to her bed, her condition rapidly deteriorating. In a traditional thatch-roof hale on the grounds of Huliheʻe Palace, Ruth Keʻelikōlani, aliʻi of old Hawaiʻi, joined her ancestors at the age of fifty-seven.

EMMA NAEA ROOKE (c. 1836–1885)

Through her mother's line, Emma Naea was the great-granddaughter of Keliʻimaikaʻi, full brother to Kamehameha. She was also a granddaughter of John Young, the British seaman who had joined Kamehameha's court in the late 1790s, becoming an aliʻi and one of the king's most trusted advisors. Adopted by her maternal aunt, Grace Kamaʻikuʻi Young Rooke, and groomed with European Victorian standards, Emma was very much an Anglo-Polynesian hybrid, sophisticated, self-possessed, well educated, and dignified. Her formal education began at the Chiefs' Children's School, a boarding school created at royal request by Amos Starr and Juliette Montague Cooke, stalwart members of the eighth American mission to Hawaiʻi, arriving in Honolulu in 1837. Two generations of highborn aliʻi attended the school, among them five future monarchs. Their education was Western in style and content, introduced with a mix of goodwill and missionary severity that contrasted with the emotional spontaneity of their aliʻi students. While some rebelled, others like Emma eagerly took to learning.

At the age of twenty, Emma entered into an initially happy marriage with Kamehameha IV, then twenty-two. Two years later she gave birth to a son,

51 | The Royal Women

Emma Naea Rooke as a young girl, with her hānai parents, British-born Dr. T. C. Rooke and Emma's aunt, Grace Kamaʻikuʻi Young.

Albert Kauikeaouli, Ka Haku o Hawaiʻi, or the Prince of Hawaiʻi, as he would come to be titled. The only royal Kamehameha of his generation, he provided the dynasty with an heir and the nation with hope for the future. The child's names had been carefully chosen. Kauikeaouli honored his grand uncle, Kamehameha III. Albert referred to Queen Victoria's prince consort, with the British royals agreeing to serve as godmother and godfather to the new prince. The link between the two royal families dated to 1849, when the teenage Alexander Liholiho and his brother had paid a visit to England, accompanied by Gerrit Judd. After their marriage, it was Emma who maintained a correspondence with the British queen, meeting her some years later, when she traveled to London to seek Victoria's support in founding an Anglican cathedral in Honolulu. Links to Britain were more than politically correct. By blood part British and raised in the home of her British uncle, Emma was thoroughly an Anglophile. Victoria's blessing barely reached the four-year-old prince in time. When her representative arrived in August 1862, Ka Haku o Hawaiʻi was dangerously ill. A quickly improvised ceremony was held. Within days he had died. "The death of no other person could have been so severe a blow to the king and his people," the newspaper reported prophetically. Little more than a year later, Kamehameha IV would also be dead, leaving Emma to grieve, a widow at twenty-seven. Emma remained in the background during much of the reign of Kamehameha V, dedicating her time to establishing a hospital to save the lives of her fast-dwindling people. Then, in 1872, Kamehameha V died without naming an heir, although Emma would later claim he had offered her the throne. Elections were held to select a new monarch and a new dynasty. Emma, Ruth Keʻelikōlani, William Lunalilo, and David Kalākaua were the four aliʻi under consideration. Lunalilo and Kalākaua were the favored choices, tradition working against the possibility of placing a reigning queen on the Hawaiian throne. Lunalilo's selection by the Legislative Assembly proved short-lived. When he died little more than one year after his election as king, Emma was once again considered for the vacant throne. This time Emma and Kalākaua were the main contenders, each actively pursuing the throne. Partisans for each side edged toward violence, for the campaign became a referendum about Native Hawaiian power and sovereignty of the kingdom, Emma representing those who claimed that there had already been enough accommodation with resident foreigners. Rallying under the banner "Hawaii for the Hawaiians" they saw Kalākaua as dangerously prone to surrendering Hawaiʻi's autonomy. Male, and of high chiefly rank, Kalākaua gained a substantial victory over Emma in the balloting in the Legislative Assembly. Emma's partisans reacted violently, several hundred rioting and attacking the electors. At Kalākaua's request, American and British troops, aboard warships anchored in Honolulu Harbor, were brought ashore to restore order, setting a precedent that would later prove ominous. Somewhat begrudgingly, Emma acknowledged Kalākaua's victory, although the threat of a coup on behalf of the dowager queen added an element of instability to the first years of Kalākaua's reign. While she would not again enter the political arena, she maintained a finger on the political pulse of the

The Royal Women | 52

islands. Emma and Kalākaua were eventually reconciled, but a letter to British Resident Commissioner James Wodehouse reveals her continuing dissatisfaction with the course of events under Kalākaua's rule:

> *The sudden and bold uncovering of America's long cherished wish...to possess these Islands... has caused me great, great grief and anxiety...I consider that America is now our open enemy...and that as we have friends in England and France, America cannot carry out her highhanded policy...The Native Hawaiians are one with me in the love of our country, and determined not to let Hawaii become apart of the United States of America...I repeat a question once put to you confidentially by a relative of mine from the Throne, Kamehameha V, whether, in case of emergency, England would take these Islands should we give ourselves up to her?*

The British response was an unequivocal no, adding substance to fears of America's emerging predominance. Despite such concerns, Emma remained apolitical for the remaining years of her life, dedicating her time to charitable and religious works. On April 25, 1885, Dowager Queen Emma, aged forty-nine, died, correctly anticipating the political turmoil that would soon overwhelm the monarchy.

Emma as queen, with the silver christening cup sent for the Prince of Hawai'i by his godparents, Queen Victoria and Prince Albert.

KAPI'OLANI (c. 1834–1899)

The granddaughter of Kaumuali'i, last king of Kaua'i, Kapi'olani was niece and namesake of the newly converted chiefess who had defied Pele in 1824, when she had stood on the crater rim of Kīlauea volcano and declared the greatness of Jehovah, not Pele.

Born in Hilo, Kapi'olani was married and a widow by the time she was twenty-six. Three years later, in 1863, she married again, in a love match to David Kalākaua. A loyal and caring couple, although of substantially different temperaments, Kalākaua often sought her advice when he became king. A romantic at heart, Kalākaua honored Kapi'olani throughout their marriage, donating the Crown Lands between Diamond Head and Waikīkī Beach as a public park named in her honor in 1877. In 1883, she shared his coronation ceremonies, being crowned as queen by Kalākaua himself.

While Kapi'olani did not play an overt political role as queen, she represented the kingdom effectively on several important occasions. Accompanied

53 | The Royal Women

Princess Liliʻuokalani had already been named heir to the throne by her brother, David Kalākaua, when she accompanied Queen Kapiʻolani (seated) to England to celebrate Queen Victoria's Jubilee.

by her sister-in-law, Liliʻuokalani, in June 1887 she attended Queen Victoria's golden jubilee in London. As a reigning queen, Kapiʻolani was accorded full royal honors throughout her visit and was well hosted and received. Prior to visiting London, Kapiʻolani stopped at Washington, D.C. to speak with President Grover Cleveland. Later, following the overthrow of the monarchy, when annexationist fervor was building in the United States, Cleveland would support Hawaiian independence, in part due to the favorable impact of Kapiʻolani's visit.

She and Kalākaua, like many other aliʻi of their generation, remained childless. Fearful for her people's survival, they worked together founding the Kapiʻolani Maternity Hospital and the Home for Leper Girls. Following Kalākaua's death in 1891, Dower Queen Kapiʻolani largely withdrew from public life. She died in 1899, six years after Liliʻuokalani had been deposed and several months short of the official annexation of Hawaiʻi.

BERNICE PAUAHI (c. 1831–1884)

Although born only twelve years after the collapse of the ancient kapu and Polynesian belief, Bernice Pauahi was very much a creation of the Victorian era, during which she came of age. Her father was the aliʻi Abner Pākī. Through her mother, Konia, she was a great-granddaughter of Kamehameha I. Well-respected for her high status, she was also well-liked by her fellow aliʻi, her people, and the world of foreigners with whom she comfortably socialized. By inclination she was too private a person to take on the prerogatives that her mana allowed her. When her cousin Kamehameha V chose her as his successor in 1872, she declined the offer. Her refusal brought to an end the Kamehameha dynasty. It was a crucial decision that ultimately affected the future course of Hawaiian history in a number of ways.

The great-granddaughter of Kamehameha I, Bernice Pauahi Bishop would have followed Kamehameha V on the throne had she accepted his deathbed offer to make her his successor. Her refusal fundamentally altered the course of Hawaiʻi's royal history.

Having inherited the bulk of the Kamehameha lands when Ruth Keʻelikōlani died in 1883, had she been Hawaiʻi's queen, she would have had the resources to pursue royal initiatives with less threat of legislative interference. Her inheritance amounted to almost one-ninth of Hawaiʻi's land and she would have reconciled the wealth of the Kamehamehas with the authority of the throne.

As a student at the Chiefs' Children's School, Pauahi absorbed a sense of missionary propriety that remained with her throughout her life. She is described as a woman of sophistication and depth, another nineteenth-century Anglo-Hawaiian hybrid aliʻi:

> Representative of the most powerful line of chiefs of olden times, Mrs. Bishop was also an exponent of the best in the foreign mode of life. Retaining a natural pride of ancestry and an interest in the welfare of her own race, she also so perfectly assimilated the spirit of Anglo-American culture [forming] a link between old and new, between Native and foreign.

A woman of high lineage, she was a logical match for the highest-born aliʻi of her generation. Courted by many, she had been betrothed to Lot Kamehameha in 1848. Before the marriage, Pauahi chose instead to marry American-born Charles Reed Bishop. One of the first of the nineteenth-century royals to wed a non-Hawaiian, her marriage started with an elopement to Kauaʻi and was marked by deep affection and loyalty, although it unfortunately brought them no children. Unlike most Americans who had settled in the islands, Bishop, who had arrived in 1846, became a naturalized citizen three years later. Establishing himself as a financier with the founding of Bishop Bank in 1858, he left much of a substantial fortune to fund the Bernice Pauahi Bishop Museum, which opened to the public in 1891. Bishop's commitment to Hawaiʻi had become obvious much earlier. Both he and his wife would serve the Hawaiian government. On October 16, 1884, Bernice Pauahi Bishop died, leaving her vast estate to benefit the Hawaiian people through the founding of the Kamehameha Schools. Committed to the well-being of her people, she had remained aloof from the social and political storms buffeting the kingdom she had refused to lead. Her passing was a milestone, for she possessed the ancestral mana of the highest aliʻi. ■

Bernice Pauahi's mother, the chiefess Konia.

Miriam Likelike, younger sister of Kalākaua and Liliʻuokalani, married Scots-born Archibald Cleghorn. Their daughter, the charismatic Kaʻiulani, would be named heir to the throne by Liliʻuokalani.

The Royal Women

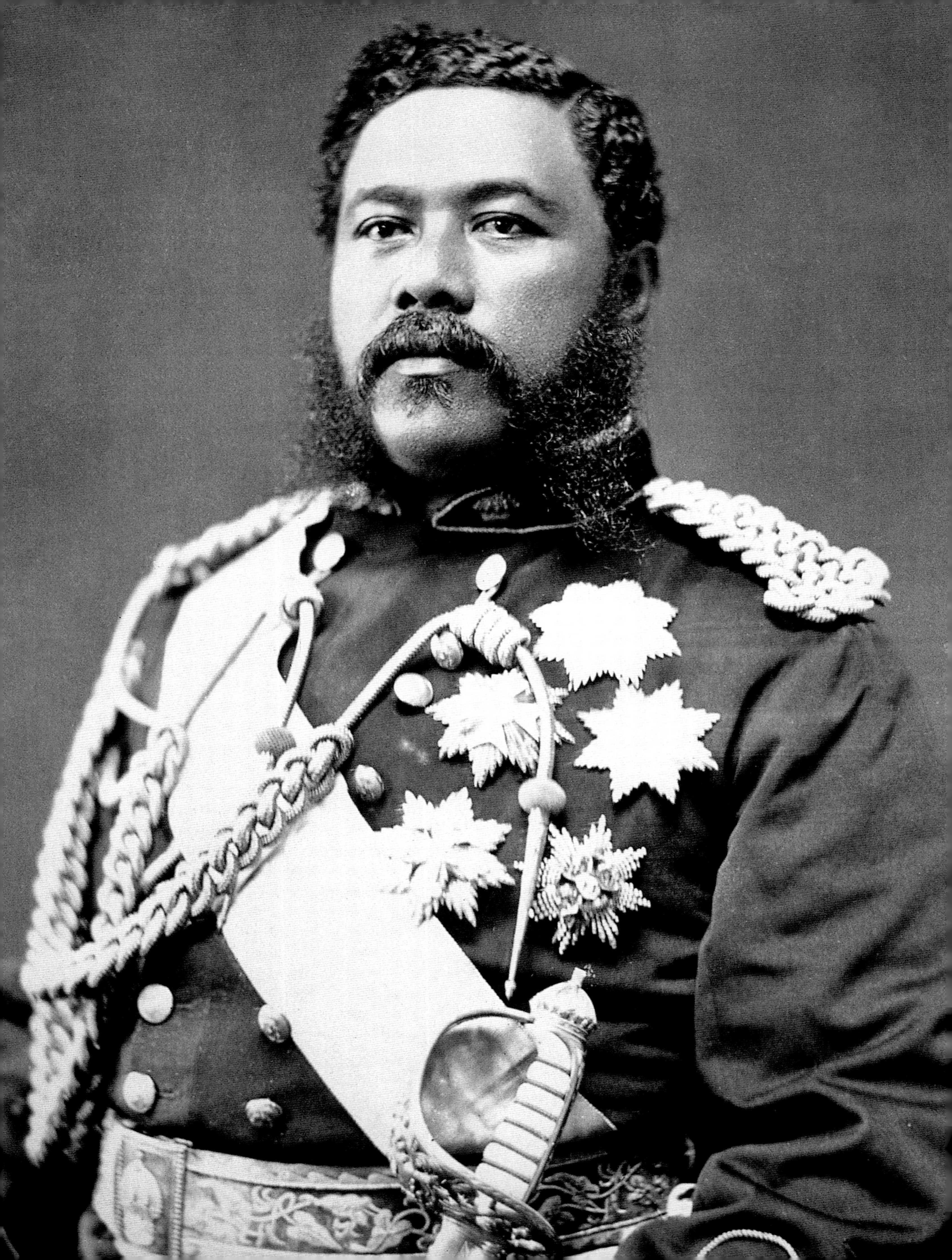

CHAPTER 10

DAVID KALĀKAUA

Strike up the band, let the hula begin (1874–1891)

Born in Honolulu in 1836, Kalākaua was educated at the missionary-run Chiefs' Children's School at a time when the old traditions still lingered. Like other royals of his generation, he was a child of two cultures. His reality was a blend of Western and Polynesian values and emotions that pitted his generous, sensitive, and spontaneous nature against the aggressive political ambitions of those increasingly hostile to monarchical rule. Trained as a lawyer and admitted to the bar in 1870, Kalākaua was sophisticated, intelligent, and observant. Having served in the House of Nobles under the last two Kamehameha kings, he was preparing himself to rule. He had firsthand experience of both the complexities of Hawaiian politics and the need for pragmatic answers to problems that long defied solution. Annexationist pressures and the depopulation of his people added a sense of urgency to events.

When King William Lunalilo died in 1874 without naming an heir, the uncertainties of succession that followed the death of Kamehameha V were repeated. An election was set for February 12, 1874, with much of the popular support that had gone to William Lunalilo now shifted to David Kalākaua. Kalākaua's opponent was Queen Emma, the pro-British aliʻi widow of Kamehameha IV, who represented anti-American sentiment. Kalākaua, they feared, lacked the resolve to confront Yankee business interests. The campaign quickly became a battle of words that focused as much on personalities as issues. Words turned to violence when the election confirmed Kalākaua as Hawaiʻi's next king. Without troops to assert his authority, Kalākaua requested that British and American sailors land to help ensure order. Although Emma's supporters withdrew, and peace was quickly restored, the rancorous feelings generated by the election lasted a decade.

Once on the throne, the king quickly acted to reestablish a legitimate ruling dynasty. He named his younger brother, the handsome William Pitt Leleiōhoku, as his heir. When

Aliʻi Caesar Kapaʻakea and Keohokālole, were parents of David Kalākaua, Lydia Kamakaʻeha (later Liliʻuokalani), Miriam Likelike (Kaʻiulani's mother), and William Pitt Leleiōhoku (later Ruth Keʻelikōlani's adopted son).

Continued on page 62

(Opposite) David La'amea Kamanakapu'u Mahinulani Naloiaehuokalani Lumialani Kalākaua—"Cry Out O Isles with Joy." The translation of Kalākaua's name becamse a hymn sung at his coronation.

On the day he became king, Kalākaua named his younger brother, William Pitt Leleiōhoku II, as heir—hoping to assure the future of his dynasty.

A stamp with Queen Emma's picture is marked with a Maltese cross, the cancellation used in the government-licensed sale of opium. When Chinese immigration swelled, the demand for opium led Kalākaua to make the licensing of opium sale to bid. The resulting financial scandal undermined Kalākaua's prestige with the foreign community.

QUEEN EMMA RECONCILING WITH KING KALĀKAUA

Following Kalākaua's tumultuous election, the king and his opponent Queen Emma attempted to heal the breach. The story of their reconciliation is told in the memoirs of Isobel Strong, an American friend of the king. Through her eyes, Kalākaua is seen as a man of chivalrous instincts, clever humor, and a flair for the dramatic. The year is 1888, the setting the USS *Adams*, at anchor in Honolulu Harbor:

We heard excited whispers "Queen Emma is here…and Kalākaua is coming. How will they meet"

…As his Majesty stepped on the deck, the ship's band burst into "Hawaii Ponoi." We, the assembled guests, opened a lane to the companionway…the men bending at the waist…the women sinking in deep curtsies as the King walked slowly along, bowing graciously to the right and left…

Breathlessly, the crowd below watched His Majesty mount the companionway; when he reached the quarter-deck…and motioned towards the Throne…where Queen Emma stood.

Kalākaua stepped forward; a gallant figure in white and gold, bowed low to the lady, in black [Emma] and offered her his hand, which she took and was about to kiss. With a quick, dextrous movement he gave her a little whirl and a push that seated her on the throne.

Queen Emma's surprised face was almost comic when the King bowed again before her. Then she smiled sweetly, he leaned over and they talked together with such evident friendliness that we all felt like applauding.

After that the two were friends…

David Kalākaua | *58*

(Top) The members of the household staff of King Kalākaua in 1887 included John Boyd, Henry Bertelman, James Robertson, and John D. Holt.

(Above) Princess Poʻomaikelani was the younger sister of Queen Kapiʻolani. Her title at court was Mistress of the Royal Robes, and during the Royal Coronation in 1883, she presented the sacred symbols of the pūloʻuloʻu, palaoa, and kāhili to the king. Later in life she served as governor of the island of Hawaiʻi.

(Left) Queen Kapiʻolani, photographed in New York in 1887 on her way to Queen Victoria's Golden Jubilee in London.

59 | David Kalākaua

After riots following his election to the throne, King Kalākaua recognized the importance of visiting his native subjects in an effort to gain their support. His frequent tours throughout the islands were always received with a great outpouring of aloha and hoʻokupu in honor of a monarch who gave his nation the goal and the motto, "Hoʻūlu Lāhui—To Increase the Race." These photos were taken during trips to Kailua-Kona and the Cook monument at Kealakekua Bay.

David Kalākaua

61 | David Kalākaua

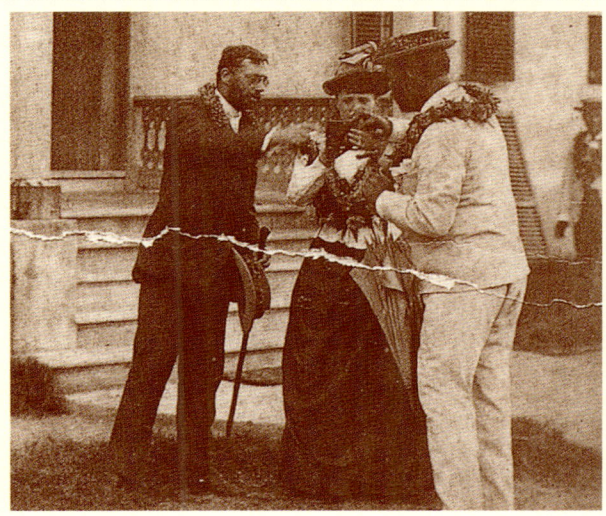

The text of "Hymn of Kamehameha I" was composed in 1874 by King Kalākaua and soon after set to music by Captain Berger of the Royal Hawaiian Band. The first public performance was by the Kawaiahaʻo Choir who sang the stately anthem on King Kalākaua's birthday in November. Two years later, the song was declared the national anthem of the Kingdom of Hawaiʻi. Played at the end of every performance of the Royal Hawaiian Band, the "Hymn of Kamehameha I" eventually became known as "Hawaiʻi Ponoʻī." Today, King Kalākaua's stirring tribute to the nation is Hawaiʻi's state song.

Continued from page 57

rheumatic fever claimed Leleiōhoku several years later at the age of twenty-two, Kalākaua chose his sister Lydia as successor, renaming her Liliʻuokalani. Having secured his dynasty, the king set out to establish his own credentials.

In March 1874, he left Honolulu for a processional tour of the kingdom, accompanied by his wife, Queen Kapiʻolani. Enlightenment was his theme, and he chose the kukui oil torch burning bright both night and day, as a symbol of his reign.

Kalākaua was deeply concerned by the dwindling native Hawaiian population, fewer than 50,000 by the mid-1870s and far too few to provide the labor required by Hawaiʻi's expanding plantation economy or to assure that Hawaiians continued sovereignty of their islands. Along with Kapiʻolani, Kalākaua sponsored the Hoʻoulu A Hoʻola Lahui Society, its name translated as "Increase the Race." In keeping with this goal, Kalākaua proposed the elimination of taxes for parents of large families and supported efforts of the Board of Health to reduce the high infant mortality rate.

The upsurge of patriotism and Hawaiian consciousness that marked the end of Lunalilo's reign and the start of Kalākaua's was seen as a threat by those foreigners with financial and political ambitions. Kalākaua, realizing the need for cooperation with the volatile American business community, traveled to Washington, D.C., in November 1874, to secure the trade advantages of reciprocity, whereby Hawaiian sugar could enter the United States duty free. Many considered the long-sought treaty that was granted in 1875 a direct result of Kalākaua's personal diplomacy and the favorable impression he made on President Grant.

To encourage immigration and promote international recognition of Hawaiian independence, King Kalākaua, on January 21, 1881, went on an around-the-world trip accompanied by Attorney General William Armstrong, Court Chamberlain Charles Judd, and his personal valet, becoming the first monarch to circle the globe. In his absence, he named his sister, Liliʻuokalani, regent.

In Japan, as the first king of a Christian nation to visit the Land of the Rising Sun, Kalākaua was treated with lavish hospitality by Emperor Mutsuhito. The issue of immigration, however, drew a negative response, as did Kalākaua's offer of marriage between his five-year-old niece Kaʻiulani and the emperor's nephew. From Japan, Kalākaua traveled to China, Thailand, India, Egypt, Italy, and Germany. By July he was in London, where he was favorably received by Queen Victoria.

Returning to Hawaiʻi after nine months of travel, Kalākaua was confronted by economic and political realities that would plague the remaining years of his reign. Internal dissent surfaced among his cabinet. Annexationist Americans, anti-monarchists, and conservative, foreign-born planters and businessmen became increasingly hostile to a monarch playing a governing role.

Having experienced the pageantry and wealth of the world's great kingdoms, and wanting "to awaken in the people, a national pride," Kalākaua set out to rally support from his people by providing symbols of sovereignty, including an elegant Victorian-style palace completed in 1882, far exceeding anything yet constructed in the Islands. Kalākaua reaffirmed his

Continued on page 66

In 1881, King Kalākaua became the first head of state to circumnavigate the globe. His journey through Asia, the Middle East, Europe, and North America included a visit with the Emperor of Japan at the Imperial Palace in Tokyo. In a private meeting, the king proposed an alliance to establish an Oceanic Empire in the Pacific. It was supposed to form a bulwark against United States encroachment on Hawai'i. The Meiji Emperor declined this intriguing suggestion, which would have radically transformed history in the Pacific. King Kalākaua was photographed sitting next to Prince Yoshiaki (left) and Yoshi Amatami, Minister of Finance (right). Standing in the second row are, from left to right: Charles H. Judd, Ryoshuki Sugai, First Secretary of Finance; and William N. Armstrong, who wrote *Around the World with a King*, a narrative of the journey.

63 | David Kalākaua

THE MERRIE MONARCH

A patron of traditional Hawaiian culture, Kalākaua was committed in more than word to a cultural renaissance. A man with broad interests and varied talents, comfortable with both polite and bawdy society, Kalākaua was well-versed in Hawaiian history, legends, and chants. In 1888, his detailed telling of ancient tales were published as *The Legends and Myths of Hawai'i*, a masterpiece of Polynesian storytelling. Two years later, the king saved from possible loss the "Kumulipo" ("Beginning-in-deep-darkness"), the Hawaiian chant of creation that is the basis of genealogical accounting. In addition, Kalākaua expanded the revival of the hula, started by Kamehameha V, after five decades of missionary-inspired prohibition. The king sponsored a royal hula troupe, introducing new dances and chants to the traditional repertoire. He also composed the lyrics for Hawai'i's anthem, "Hawai'i Pono'i," sponsored the Royal Hawaiian Band and developed virtuoso skills on the newly introduced 'ukulele. If there was greatness in Kalākaua, it was in his commitment to restoring the cultural legacy of his people just as it was on the verge of being lost.

This 1889 lū'au, or feast, at Manuia Lanai, the Waikīkī residence of Henry Poor, honored the world-famous author Robert Louis Stevenson. Suffering from tuberculosis, the Scottish author of *Treasure Island, Dr. Jekyll and Mr. Hyde,* and *Kidnapped* left San Francisco in 1888 with his wife, mother, and stepson on the schooner *Casco* for an extended voyage. After visiting the Marquesas Islands, Fakarava Atoll, and Tahiti, Stevenson and his family arrived in Hawai'i for a six-month sojourn. Soon he met Poor, a secretary in the Kalākaua government and the future charge d'affaires to Samoa.

Attending the lavish Hawaiian feast were (seated from left, clockwise): the Island artist Joseph Strong, Robert Louis Stevenson, Princess Lili'uokalani, King Kalākaua, Mrs. Thomas Stevenson (the author's mother), Mrs. Fanny Osbourne Stevenson (his wife), Henry Poor, Mrs. Isobel Osbourne Strong (wife of Joseph Strong and stepdaughter of Stevenson).

During the festivities, Fanny Stevenson presented the king with a rare golden pearl. This was followed by the author giving him another pearl and one of only three poems he ever wrote about Hawai'i. "The ocean jewel," the verse ends, "to the island king."

David Kalākaua

King Kalākaua's reputation for enjoying soirées, dances, drinking, horse racing, lavish parties and gambling—although often exaggerated by his enemies—was not without basis. The king had a robust temperament which would not be restrained by the prudery of his missionary teachers, for whom he felt a healthy measure of contempt. Far from the watchful eyes of what he called "our miserable bigoted community" of Church members who were "all sober and down in the mouth," Kalākaua entertained friends and visitors at the Royal Boat House at the harbor.

(Right) There his guests such as Lloyd Osbourne (left) and Robert Louis Stevenson (center) found the king a gracious, well-read, and convivial host, who into the early morning hours enjoyed a hand of cards on his poker table with the royal crest.

(Right) One of Kalākaua's greatest contributions was the revival of ancient Hawaiian art forms such as the hula. If Kalākaua failed politically, he did much to restore pride in Hawaiian culture.

65 | David Kalākaua

Continued from page 62

rule by scheduling a coronation for February 12, 1883, the ninth anniversary of his accession to the throne. Festooned with the medals and royal orders he had received during his travels abroad, the king made his appearance accompanied by Queen Kapiʻolani. The ceremonial regalia was an eclectic blend of ancient Hawaiian and contemporary European. Most impressive were the yellow feather cloak of the first Kamehameha, the kāhili, the kukui torch symbolic of the Kalākaua dynasty, the sword of state, scepter, ring, and two crowns of gemstones and gold. The ceremony ended with Kalākaua crowning himself and his queen.

Thousands of people attended, and thousands more enjoyed the two weeks of festivities that culminated in a grand public lūʻau and the Coronation Ball. However, the reformists quickly condemned the expenditure of more than $50,000 on what they judged a personal extravagance.

Neither the king nor the legislature seemed capable of the fiscal restraint that the nation's limited resources demanded. Much of the financing for the soaring national debt came from loans made to the government by sugar millionaire Claus Spreckels, a German-born, American-made entrepreneur with a robber-baron mentality. By 1886, the Hawaiian government was $2 million in his debt, and the integrity of the monarchy was being openly questioned.

The Missionary Party blamed the king and the Native Hawaiian legislators for this sorry state of affairs. A political showdown followed that led to Spreckels leaving for California. The following year, all debts were paid from bonds floated by the government. More punishing though was the damage to Kalākaua's credibility and prestige.

Early in 1887, a secret political organization called The Hawaiian League was formed. While one faction of the League called for reform via constitutional changes limiting the king's authority, another called for the abolition of the monarchy and eventual annexation of Hawaiʻi to the United States. The League, whose members were mostly foreign-born or nonnative citizens of the kingdom, was led by an executive organization commonly called the Committee of Thirteen. In effect, the league provided the Missionary Party with political clout supported by three companies of the Honolulu Rifles, an extra-governmental regiment made up mostly of non-native volunteers.

By June, with the king's astute prime minister, Walter Murray Gibson, unpopular with reformists, succumbing to ill health, events took a turn for the worse. Fearing an outright attack, Kalākaua fortified the palace with five military units of native Hawaiian and part-native troops. Advised by the United States minister, Kalākaua called for the resignation of his cabinet at a midnight meeting on June 28. The move came too late to silence the opposition. Demands for changes in the constitution led to the inevitable calls for an end to the monarchy. Understanding his vulnerability, Kalākaua met with representatives of the United States, Great Britain, France, Portugal, and Japan hoping to place the affairs of the kingdom in their hands thereby undermining the position of the League. His request fell on deaf ears. By July 8, 1887, realizing the futility of resistance, Kalākaua

February 12, 1883, Kalākaua crowns himself king in an elaborate coronation ceremony on the grounds of newly completed ʻIolani Palace.

FEBRUARY 12, 1883
THE CORONATION OF A KING

"On the day of the Coronation," wrote Isobel Strong Field, stepdaughter of Robert Louis Stevenson, "natives passed our house in eager groups, dressed in their best... We saw silken holokus of every color, the long trains thrown over the arm; all hats were garlanded with flowers and every neck was encircled with a bright golden lei...It was a glorious day, sunny and vivid, with the cool breath of the sea that makes the climate of the islands so perfect.

"A huge throng gathered on the grounds of recently completed 'Iolani Palace. The grand edifice, a showcase for the royal Hawaiian family, had been built under the direction of King Kalākaua. Four thousand guests sat in chairs around the special Coronation Pavilion festooned with banners, flags and flowers. Four thousand more onlookers stood farther back. Two thrones awaited the royal couple. Across the street the newly unveiled statue of King Kamehameha gleamed golden in the morning sun. The ceremony commenced with the Royal Hawaiian Band performing *Hawai'i Pono'ī*, the new national anthem.

"His Majesty first placed a magnificent, jewel-bedecked crown on the head of his consort, Queen Kapi'olani. Then pronouncing himself King Kalākaua of the Hawaiian Islands, he placed his own crown upon his head. Following the ceremony, ancient hula dances were performed in honor of the occasion throughout the day and into the night. The spectacular festivities had a sense of royal grandeur inspired by a Hawaiian visionary who sought to restore the pride and spirit of his race."

67 | David Kalākaua

accepted a reform cabinet chosen by the League that did not include a single native Hawaiian member. It operated independently of the king, setting its own agenda and initiating its own legislation. With reformists in control of the legislature, a new constitution containing a series of fiscal and administrative restraints reduced the king to a figurehead. The Bayonet Constitution, as it came to be called, forced a financial and political surrender on the king.

Kalākaua fought back, focusing his energies on a court filing that claimed his rights had been unconstitutionally compromised. The court decided in the king's favor, and was supported by royalists who felt the reformers were going too far.

The reformist government, seeking ways to take control of the budget and stymie Kalākaua's independence, eliminated the royal stipend, and scheduled new legislative elections for later in the year. The election took place in February under the watchful eye of the British and the Americans, whose warships were anchored offshore. Surprisingly, the vote proved a setback for the reformists, and Kalākaua remained on the throne.

During the seventeen years that had passed since Kalākaua began his rule the stability of the Hawaiian Kingdom had changed for the worse. Much that Kalākaua set out to accomplish remained unresolved. Hawai'i's independence was being severely threatened by the decisions of foreign governments and foreign-born businessmen. Although the population of the islands had begun to increase, due to an influx of 55,000 foreign workers, the Native Hawaiian population continued its precipitous decline. The 1890 census counted 35,000 Native Hawaiians, about 15,000 fewer than when Kalākaua came to the throne. The Hawaiians were now a minority in their own kingdom. As the native population weakened, so did the kingdom's grassroots support. Also gone were a whole generation of ali'i, including Ruth Ke'elikōlani and Bernice Pauahi Bishop, last of the highborn Kamehamehas, who died in 1881 and 1883 respectively; Queen Emma, who died in 1885; Kalākaua's brother Leleiōhoku, who died in 1877; and his sister, Miriam Likelike, who died early in 1887. His health in decline, Kalākaua left Honolulu for San Francisco in late November, hoping a change of setting and medical attention might restore him. That hope quickly faded.

The end came quickly: a mild stroke in January gave way to kidney failure and an attack of cirrhosis. On January 20, 1891, King Kalākaua died in his hotel room at the age of fifty-four. The U.S. naval ship *Charleston* departed San Francisco with the king's body aboard. When it docked in Honolulu several days later, flags set at half-mast revealed to those gathered to welcome the king home that something was amiss. According to an eyewitness account:

> *Gloom spread where all had been so gay. Colorful decorations were hastily removed, giving place to sombre black. Now the barge from the* Charleston *neared the landing. From the crowd emerged a white haired Hawaiian woman. She was thin and bent and barefoot. She wore a neat black holoku and an old fashioned hat of Hawaiian lauhala braid. Unassisted, she climbed to the top of the largest pile of coal* [steam ships used coal as fuel].

There she stood, a slender, dark silhouette against the clear sunny sky. Now the coffin was lifted from the barge. With a queenly, graceful motion, she raised her right arm high above her head. Then in the rich resonant voice of the Polynesian, she began to wail. Syllables gushed over syllables in the soft Hawaiian language, as she eulogized Kalākaua and recounted the deeds of his ancestors. The coffin was reverently placed upon a horsedrawn truck that had been suitably draped. With its escort the vehicle headed for the Palace in a scene described by Hayden Treadway:

> *...the sky was clear and bright with no sign of mist. I looked up and saw that we were walking directly toward the arch of the grandest, brightest rainbow [considered a symbol of royalty] that I had ever seen.*
>
> *The procession took a right turn yet directly in front of us was the rainbow. It remained undimmed. The splendid arch still faced us as we turned our way toward Kaimuki, exactly opposite from the position where it had first appeared...The beautiful rainbow maintained its watch until dusk. "Auwe!" cried the people. "He ali'i oia i'o no ka o Kalākaua!" Kalākaua is indeed an ali'i.* ■

On February 15, 1891, the funeral procession of King Kalākaua moved solemnly down King Street as his native subjects carried large kāhili, or feather standards, on all four sides of the koa wood casket, partially draped in a magnificent yellow feather cape. The King's Guard, several military companies, Hawaiian legislators, and the fraternal societies of the kingdom marched in measured cadence as Queen Kapi'olani rode in a closed and shrouded carriage behind her husband's casket.

(Above, left) Queen Kapi'olani knelt in prayer at the casket of King Kalākaua, which lay in state for over two weeks in the Throne Room of 'Iolani Palace.

(Above, right) King Kalākaua's remains were laid to rest at the Royal Mausoleum at Mauna 'Ala in Nu'uanu Valley. The committal service was conducted by Bishop Alfred Willis of the Anglican Church, followed by a burial service held by members of the Masonic fraternity, of which Kalākaua had been a faithful member.

69 | David Kalākaua

ROBERT WILCOX

Kalākaua founded the King's Guards to replace the Royal Household Troops disbanded by Lunalilo. Understanding the need for a defensive military force, Kalākaua seems to have been planning an expansion of his militia, sending several Hawaiian-born students for military school training in Europe, where they stayed until recalled in 1887, when the Bayonet Constitution cut the royal purse strings.

Robert Wilcox, a free-spirited part-Hawaiian of ali'i descent, was one of these young people. Wilcox had been living in Italy and studying military science for six years at the king's expense. In 1887, he, along with twenty-six other Hawaiian youth, were forced to return to the islands.

Committed to preserving Hawaiian independence, as a monarchy, if possible, but as a republic should circumstances call for more radical change, Wilcox established the secret Liberal Patriotic Society. Its mission was to remove the reformist government and restore true authority to the crown. Wilcox secretly helped organize the Kamehameha Rifles, a royalist counterpart to the Honolulu Rifles.

On the morning of July 30, armed with rifles, pistols, and bird guns, Wilcox and about eighty followers gained access to the 'Iolani Palace grounds. It is uncertain if Kalākaua supported those who acted in his name in seeking to overthrow the Bayonet Constitution. Hearing of Wilcox's action, the government posted sharpshooters in buildings surrounding the Palace. By afternoon it was over, Wilcox was captured after a mid-day battle that saw seven royalists killed. Few of those arrested ever went on trial, as the government realized the difficulty of gaining convictions of men considered heroes by the majority of native Hawaiians. Even Wilcox, against whom the evidence was conclusive, was acquitted at his trial. To assure no repetition of the Wilcox insurrection, the government responded by further restraining the autonomy of the king, removing weaponry from the Palace compound, reducing the size of the King's Guard, and asserting the cabinet's administrative autonomy and executive primacy.

WALTER MURRAY GIBSON

King Kalākaua appointed the controversial Walter Murray Gibson as premier and minister of foreign affairs. Gibson was the king's strongest supporter, with a forceful personality willing to confront the kingdom's enemies. American-born (actually born at sea when his parents were en route from England to America), Gibson was a free-spirited idealist and self-proclaimed defender of the Hawaiian Kingdom. Having failed in his effort at creating an agricultural commune on Lāna'i, Gibson moved to Honolulu, ideals intact, to serve in the legislature. Kalākaua was attracted to the charismatic Gibson's visionary goals. For nine stormy years, Gibson charted the course of the royal government, creating an ever-deeper divide between those in support of the king and those in opposition. Many looked upon Gibson as the source of Kalākaua's ruin. They claimed that his policies played into Kalākaua's modestly Napoleonic personality, inspiring in him political ambitions and grandiose plans out of keeping with the resources of his kingdom.

KALĀKAUA'S DREAM OF A POLYNESIAN EMPIRE

In 1886 Kalākaua sent John Bush, a part-Hawaiian, to Samoa as envoy extraordinary and high commissioner to the sovereign chiefs and peoples of Polynesia. Bush was instructed to pursue an alliance with Samoan chief Malietoa that would place Samoa under Hawaiian hegemony. Similar alliances would then be proposed to other independent islands of the Polynesian Pacific. The American minister in Honolulu wrote of Kalākaua's intentions: "I know from conversations with the King...that his imagination is inflamed with the idea of gathering all the cognate races of the Islands of the Pacific into a great Polynesian Confederacy, over which he will reign."

An editorial in 1883 in the *Pacific Commercial Advertiser* supported Kalākaua's imperial ambitions:

> There is no...good reason why the islands of the South Pacific should become appendages of distant powers...If any one is to interfere to prevent further aggrandizing of foreign and distant powers in the Pacific, Hawaii ought to do it.

Chief Malietoa, his right to speak for the Samoan people contested by civil war, agreed to Kalākaua's proposal. In mid-June, the newly commissioned Hawaiian navy, consisting of a single, recently converted copra trader, reached Apia on the Samoan island of Upolu to promote Kalākaua's plans for a Polynesian confederation. By late September, however, Kalākaua had to face reality, for the Germans were also committed to securing a colonial empire, with Samoa already chosen as a mid-Pacific outpost. They responded quickly to Kalākaua's proposed confederacy, issuing a terse statement that any efforts to pursue his goals in Samoa would put him in a state of war with Germany. The threat achieved its goal when Germany and the United States made a division of Samoa without even advising the Hawaiian government.

Kalākaua aboard the steamer *Ka 'Imiloa* ("the far seeker") just before it set out for Samoa in 1887. The king sent a mission to Samoa seeking to form a pan-Polynesian kingdom with Kalākaua as its head. The drunken behavior of Kalākaua's part-Hawaiian representative, John Bush, alienated many of the Samoan chiefs. Foreign powers with their own colonial agendas quickly nixed the project.

David Kalākaua

KAMEHAMEHA EHUNA, KA MOI

KAMEHAMEHA I

CHAPTER 11

✶ ROYAL RESIDENCES ✶

Due to the outdoor lifestyle, residential architecture was not a monumental or elaborate art form in old Hawai'i. Even the homes of the ali'i were not elaborate, being slightly upgraded versions of the thatched-roof hale pictured in early views of the islands. Hale were simple structures with no windows, and usually only one or two small doors cut purposefully low to humble all who entered. Houses were named, providing them a spiritual identity.

A high chief's household was a compound of separate hale, each serving a specific function. The more important the chief, the more buildings were part of the kauhale, or royal compound. The floor of each house was covered in finely plaited lauhala mats, with a small, walled fireplace positioned in the center of the room that was kept burning, more to keep away night-roaming spirits than for warmth. The hale moe, or sleeping house, provided a central residence for the chiefly family. The bed was a pile of finely-plaited makaloa mats atop a raised platform which allowed the chief and chiefess to sleep above all others. When called a hale noa, the house was considered free of kapu, which in most social contexts kept men and women apart. Food was not brought into the sleeping house, which also served as a place for socializing with family and friends. The hale mua, or men's eating house, was very strictly segregated, off-limits to women as well as men of lesser rank. The 'ai kapu, which related to food and eating, were in force here. The natives rigidly adhered to these kapu, for they were considered sacred, decreed by the gods, not by men. Pūlo'ulo'u, or kapu sticks, stood outside the hale mua warning the uninvited of the presence of ali'i. Within the hale mua, the chief offered daily prayers and food to his 'aumakua, the family gods, at an altar at one end of the hale. Women would eat and socialize in their own eating house called the hale 'āina, where they were also confined during the menstrual period. Within the kauhale, there were also ho'āhu, storehouses for food crops collected at makahiki. These wood and thatch structures were usually built several feet above the ground on fitted wooden planks. If the kauhale lay near the sea, it might well include a halau wa'a, a large, open-sided shed for canoes. Similar in construction were the halau hula, for instruction in sacred dances, and the halau lua, for wrestling matches.

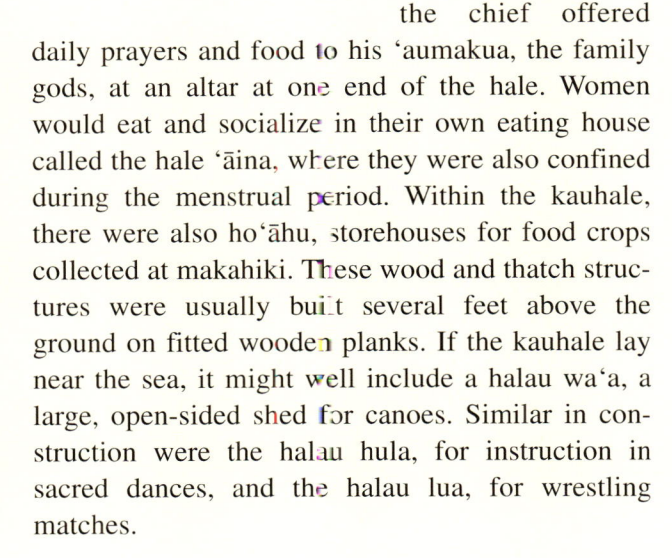

Five monarchs occupied the first 'Iolani Palace, built between 1844–46 on the location where the current 'Iolani Palace stands. It was torn down after more than thirty years in use, replaced by Kalākaua's distinctive Victorian mansion also called 'Iolani, "hawk of heaven."

(Opposite) Kamehameha IV commissioned the building of Ali'iōlani Hale as a new residence for Hawai'i's rulers; but he died in 1863, before construction began. Not being interested in building a palace, Kamehameha V changed the purpose of the building to that of an administrative center. He laid the cornerstone in 1872; the building was completed during Lunalilo's reign; and Kalākaua opened Ali'iōlani Hale, 1874, to house the Royal Legislature, Hawai'i's courts, and some ministries.

In this 1826 watercolor, *View Near the Town of Honoruru, Sandwich Islands, From the Taro Patches* by Richard Beechey, the peaked roof thatch-covered houses in the center foreground are an aliʻi compound.

Kamehameha I lived like a traditional aliʻi nui. His royal compound, surrounded by lava rock walls, also included a heiau called Ahuʻena, with an altar dedicated to the Kamehameha family gods.

Halehui, the first royal residence of the Hawaiian Kingdom, was built on the shores of Waikīkī following Kamehameha's conquest of Oʻahu in 1795. For fifteen years, he intermittently ruled from this traditional kauhale. While most of the walled-in compound was constructed in the old style, there were two stone repositories of Western design, where Kamehameha stored the king's growing accumulation of trade goods. Later in his reign, when he temporarily moved the capital to Lāhainā, he built a two-story brick residence, more Western than Polynesian in design. Kamehameha's final years were spent on the island of Hawaiʻi at Kailua-Kona, on land claimed through his father's line. Here he built a large compound that consisted of traditional-style homes for his wives, and warehouses of Western construction. It was in Kamakahonu, the kauhale that Kamehameha called "the eye of the turtle," that the great king died in 1819.

Kamehameha II built a hybrid hale of lumber and thatch at a favored canoe landing facing Honolulu Harbor called Pākākā ("skimming stones over the water"). A missionary visitor described the building as fifty-feet long, thirty-feet wide, and thirty feet high where the thatch peaked. Its timbers were tall, straight, and beautifully hewn, lashed together with sennit rope. Pākākā was a building of modified Western design with two large doors at either end, and large Venetian windows that opened to the harbor.

Kamehameha III's residence was originally built by Boki, the young chief who had accompanied Kamehameha II to London in 1823. It, too, featured a hybrid of timber and thatch, built on a walled parcel of several acres not far from where ʻIolani Palace stands today. The main house, called Haleuluhe ("house of uluhe ferns"), was a substantial building one hundred feet long and nearly sixty feet wide, with a pili grass thatch that peaked at forty feet. An edging of brown uluhe ferns ornamented the exterior. Interior posts were tied in intricately patterned sennit cord, and the floor was paved with stone and mortar, then covered with finely woven mats. Glass doors, the first in the Islands, were decorated with crimson damask. Portraits of Kamehameha II and Queen Kamāmalu, painted in London, hung on the wall, illuminated by crystal chandeliers. The throne was a carved-wood armchair draped with the yellow feather cloak of Kamehameha I, a symbol of the royal past. In 1836, Kamehameha III moved his court from Haleuluhe to

Royal Residences | 74

Sketch by Louis Choris, 1817, of a chiefly gathering inside the simply furnished, womb-like interior of a thatch structure described as being "a handsome room thirty by fifty feet and rising thirty feet high at the peak with beautifully hewn timbers..." The reclining chief is said to be Liholiho, who would become Kamehameha II in 1819.

Halekauwila ("house of kauwila wood"), built near the fort that dominated Honolulu Harbor. People believed the house to be sacred because of the timbers used in its construction. Kaʻahumanu recovered the wood from the sacred Hale-o-Keawe at Hōnaunau, where the bones of the king's royal ancestors were once stored and venerated. An innovative use of sliding screens allowed the sixty-by-forty-foot salon to be divided into smaller rooms. When the court moved from Honolulu to Lāhainā in 1838, the royal workers built a new residence of cut coral blocks. Called Hale Piula ("house of the metal roof"), it was fully Westernized, complete with wraparound lānai and a red tin roof. When the king returned to Honolulu in 1845, a cottage-style residence, later called ʻIolani ("hawk of heaven") was built for him. This colonial-style, single-story building was richly carpeted, with furnishings of koa wood in Victorian design. Service was of goldplate and silver, accompanied by fine glassware and the best imported

Kamehameha III's royal compound (far right) in Honolulu in 1826. His later residences incorporated Western buildings as part of the royal compound.

In 1845 he had a Western-style residence built. This hale aliʻi (royal palace) was named ʻIolani in 1863 by Kamehameha V, who named it in honor of his recently deceased brother, Kamehameha IV. The first ʻIolani Palace was demolished in 1878 by King Kalākaua and was replaced by the current palace bearing the same name (see page 73).

75 | Royal Residences

china. Several kāhili and two feather cloaks from Kamehameha I provided the essential link to the past.

Iolani served as a royal residence for more than thirty years, surrendering to use and termites just in time for Kalākaua to plan a grand Victorian mansion for the site, also called 'Iolani. Built over a span of three years, at a cost of $350,000, 'Iolani Palace provided Kalākaua with a showpiece for his kingdom. The cornerstone for the architecturally distinguished building was laid on December 31, 1879, timed to coincide with Queen Kapi'olani's birthday. The royal couple moved in nearly three years later, establishing residence as the finishing touches were being completed. 'Iolani Palace served as headquarters for the executive branch of a sovereign government, a symbol of Hawaiian autonomy and royal authority. Four stories high, 'Iolani Palace retains its belle epoque charm. Interiors are rich in polished woods, with details befitting a Victorian mansion. The palace officially opened in February 1883, when Kalākaua hosted thousands at a coronation on the palace grounds. The two weeks of celebrations that followed cost the treasury another $50,000. For Kalākaua it was part ego and part a matter of fulfilling his obligation as an ali'i. "Ho'ipu'olo no o kahiali'i," a Hawaiian proverb says, "One returns with a bundle from the place of the chief." A chief was expected to be generous. Wealth and generosity were signs of enhanced mana. But, in the eyes of the political opposition, 'Iolani Palace was proof of fiscal irresponsibility and imperial posturing.

For most of the century that followed—years as a monarchy, a provisional government, a republic, a territory and a state—'Iolani Palace has served as the seat of government. Beautifully restored under the auspices of the Friends of 'Iolani Palace, this home of ali'i has become a treasured symbol of Hawai'i's royal past.

Washington Place, near 'Iolani Palace also served as a royal residence. Built between 1842 and 1846 by the American merchant ship captain John Dominis, it became a symbol of royalty after the monarchy was overthrown in 1893. It was here that Queen Lili'uokalani, wife of Dominis' son, John Owen, spent most of the twenty-four years that followed her forced abdication. The monarchical era came to an end in this home on November 11, 1917, when Lili'uokalani, frail and venerable, died at age seventy-nine. Today, after many years as the Governor's Mansion, Washington Place is open to the public. ■

Completed in 1838 and built of lava rock and coral mortar, the two-story, New England-style residence called Hulihe'e (literally, "turn and flee") was built by John Adams Kuakini, brother of Ka'ahumanu and governor of the island of Hawai'i. Hulihe'e sits on an oceanfront portion of Kamehameha I's royal compound, inherited by Ruth Ke'elikōlani in the 1850s. It served as a residence for royals visiting Kailua-Kona, including Kamehameha IV, Lunalilo, and Kalākaua. Kalākaua bought the property after Ruth's death in 1883, furnishing the simple frame house in Victorian excess. The house was nearly in ruins by 1925 when the Daughters of Hawai'i rescued, restored, and refurnished it, creating a small museum with links to Hawai'i's monarchical century.

ALI'IŌLANI HALE

This "house of a chief known unto the heavens" was originally planned as a residence for Kamehameha V. Designed in 1869, the plan was changed when the king suggested that it instead be used by the legislature, courts, and ministries. So it was, opening its doors in 1874. It remains a lovely downtown landmark, backdrop to the bronze statue of Kamehameha as the warrior king. Ali'iōlani Hale was the first government building of architectural stature and impact.

HĀNAIAKAMALAMA

Landscaped grounds surround Hānaiakamalama ("the foster child of the moon"), Queen Emma's country home, located in the cool reaches of Nu'uanu Valley. Built between 1843 and 1849 at a cost of $6,000, the one-story home was the favored country residence of Kamehameha IV and Queen Emma. Emma inherited it from her uncle, Keoni Ana, who served in the Hawaiian government during the reign of Kamehameha III and had inherited it from his mother, Mary Ka'ō'ana'eha, ali'i wife of British seaman John Young. The royal couple added a room to the residence in 1869, in expectation of a visit by Queen Victoria's second son, Alfred, the Duke of Edinburgh. The British prince never arrived, but the room was soon put to good use after the birth of the Prince of Hawai'i, who spent much of his short life there. After 1872, Emma never stayed at Hānaiakamalama. Falling into ruin, the house was rescued from demolition in 1913 by the Daughters of Hawai'i, who restored it and opened it to the public in 1915. It is now known as Queen Emma's Summer Palace.

(Left) The stately Hānaiakamalama (c. 1848), was the Nu'uanu Valley home of John Young II (or John Young, Jr., also known as Keoni Ana). He was the son of an Englishman of the same name, who was also known as Keoni Ana. The son served in the Hawaiian government during the reign of Kamehameha III. When Keoni Ana died, 1857, Queen Emma—his favorite niece—inherited the house. (Above) Today the lovely, high-ceilinged Victorian home is a historic site preserved as Queen Emma's Summer Palace.

Royal Residences

KEŌUAHALE

As if to assert the wealth of the Kamehamehas against that of the reigning Kalākauas, Princess Ruth Keʻelikōlani, heir to most of the lands granted the Kamehamehas during the Great Māhele of 1848, built an ornate Victorian mansion not far from ʻIolani Palace. Called Keōuahale (Keōua House), it opened with great fanfare in February 1882, while ʻIolani Palace was still under construction. Great irony attached itself to this palatial home that was so out of keeping with Ruth's persona. The house, perhaps designed to introduce Ruth to the Victorian Age, proved to be her swan song. The opening of Keōuahale was celebrated with a lavish lūʻau attended by hundreds. After living in her new home for two days she took ill and headed by steamer to the island of Hawaiʻi. Ruth died in Kailua-Kona, not in her grand Victorian mansion, but in a traditional pili-thatched house on the grounds of Huliheʻe Palace. Keōuahale passed on to Bernice Pauahi, who used it as her primary residence until her death in 1884. The house was returned to Pauahi's estate by her husband in 1894, and sold for $30,000 to the Board of Education as a school. Deemed structurally unsafe after forty years, it was razed in 1925 and replaced by the far less distinguished Central Intermediate School.

(Above) Although Princess Ruth Keʻelikōlani built herself a Victorian mansion, called Keōuahale ("House of Keōua") in Honolulu, she lived there only three nights. Falling ill following the opening reception for her new home, she returned to the island of Hawaiʻi where she died in a traditional thatch-roofed hale adjacent to Huliheʻe Palace.

Royal Residences | 78

As a prince, Lot (Kamehameha V) had a vacation place in Moanalua on Oʻahu. When he became king, a green summer house cottage, named for him, was built there in the midst of a large garden in 1867. Here he held lūʻau gatherings and hula performances and invited important travelers between Honolulu and ʻEwa to rest. Today, these lands are known as "Moanalua Gardens." They are owned and maintained by the Samuel M. Damon Estate but kept open for use by the public. The Prince Lot Hula Festival is held in the gardens on the third Sunday in July each year to honor the prince.

Kamehameha V had several homes, including a lovely bungalow in the midst of a palm grove in Waikīkī, where the Royal Hawaiian Hotel now stands. He also had a country home built on the lowlands at Moanalua in an eclectic mix of Hawaiian, Oriental, and Victorian styles.

Royal Residences

John I'i was educated at Lāhaināluna Seminary, the missionary school established to prepare Hawaiians for teaching and entry into the ministry. I'i became an advisor to Hiram Bingham, a teacher at the Chiefs' Children's School, a counselor to the government of Kamehameha III and a judge on the superior court. An ardent proponent of Hawaiian independence, he spoke out strongly against American annexation when it was proposed by the government in 1854.

(Left) Hawaiian chief Abner Pākī served as the captain of Honolulu Fort in 1840 and, during his distinguished governmental career, was also a Supreme Court judge, member of the House of Nobles, acting governor of O'ahu, privy counselor and chamberlain to Kamehameha III. He married Konia, a granddaughter of Kamehameha I and member of the legislature from 1840–1847. In 1831, the couple had a daughter, Princess Bernice Pauahi, who was destined to be the last Kamehameha heir. They were also hānai parents to Lili'u Kamaka'eha, later Queen Lili'uokalani. In 1847, Pākī built a large house in Nu'uanu which he named Haleakalā. After his death in 1855, it became the home of the princess and her American husband, banker Charles Reed Bishop.

Royal Residences | *80*

Washington Place was an American Georgian manor built by Capt. John Dominis in 1846. One year later he sailed to China to buy furnishings for his new home, and was lost at sea. His widow, Mary Dominis, and son, John Owen, rented out some of the twelve rooms to supplement their income. After obtaining permission from Kamehameha III, the house was named Washington Place by U.S. Commissioner Anthony Ten Eyck, a resident at the time. John Owen Dominis later married Princess Lili'uokalani, who, in her last years, found solace behind the walls of Washington Place. Long the official residence of the governor of Hawai'i, it is now open to the public.

(Right) In 1850, Princess Bernice Pauahi renounced her betrothal to Prince Lot Kamehameha to marry a New Yorker, Charles Reed Bishop. The young newlyweds may have occupied this modest home in 1854, but Bishop soon became one of the wealthiest financiers in the Islands. In 1858, he established the Bishop Bank, the first and, for many years, the only institution of its kind in the kingdom.

Lithographs on these two pages are from drawings by Swiss artist Paul Emmert in the 1850s.

Royal Residences

WAIKĪKĪ: ROYAL PLAYGROUND

After bringing Oʻahu under his rule, Kamehameha I recognized the importance of Waikīkī by placing his royal compound at Ulukou, a sacred chiefly area which a century later became the site of the Moana Hotel.

Later, as foreign ships began to use Honolulu Harbor, the court was established nearby to be able to monitor trade, although the king maintained his Waikīkī residence.

The quiet solitude of Waikīkī continued to attract the royal families of the nineteenth century who sought a retreat from Honolulu's hustle and bustle and the severe, watchful eye of the American Protestant missionaries at Kawaiahaʻo. Kamehameha V built his cottage in 1866 among the famed 10,000 coconut trees of the King's Grove at Helumoa, the site of an ancient heiau used for makahiki celebrations. In July 1869, Prince Alfred Ernest Albert, second son of Queen Victoria, attended a large lūʻau at Hamohamo, the Waikīkī home of Mrs. Lydia Dominis, the future Queen Liliʻuokalani. During the festivities, an exhibition of hula was performed far from the scornful gaze of Honolulu's religious leaders.

The lure of cooling winds among the palm-lined shores and time spent bathing in nurturing seas was irresistible to members of the Kamehameha and Kalākaua dynasties who built cottage retreats at Waikīkī. With Diamond Head as a backdrop, reef-sheltered waters the color of melted aquamarines and gentle breezes to rustle the palms, Waikīkī proved a perfect royal retreat.

King Kalākaua often used Uluniu, his Waikīkī home which he obtained in 1880, as a comfortable retreat for parties and extended rests.

Circa 1880, the Waikīkī home of Princess Bernice Pauahi Bishop was on the Kamehameha lands at Helumoa.

Royal Residences | *82*

(Top) King Lunalilo's Waikīkī residence was later inherited by Queen Emma following the king's death in 1874. Today the grounds are the site of the International Marketplace on Kalākaua Avenue. (Bottom left) King Kamehameha V's grass-thatched cottage was located among the famous 10,000 coconut trees of Helumoa. The Seaside Hotel and later the Royal Hawaiian Hotel were built on these grounds. (Bottom right) When Princess Victoria Ka'iulani was baptized in 1875, her godmother, Princess Ruth Ke'elikōlani, gave her the lands of 'Āinahau at Waikīkī. Its ten acres were extensively landscaped by Princess Ka'iulani's father, who also supervised the construction of a two-story, white frame house for the family. The famed banyan tree nearby, photographed in 1890, was immortalized in a poem to the princess by Robert Louis Stevenson.

83 | Royal Residences

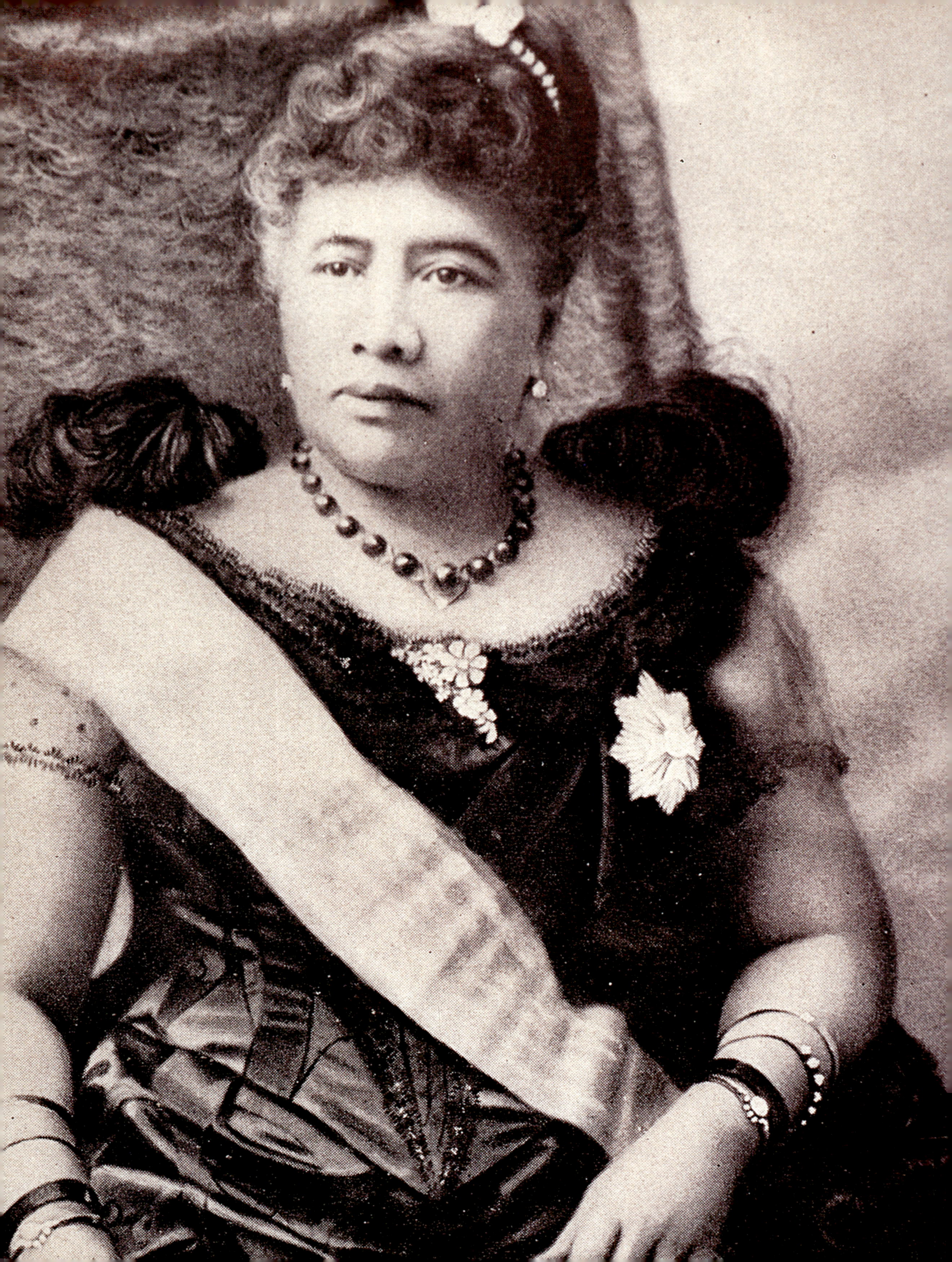

CHAPTER 12

LYDIA KAMAKA'EHA / LILI'UOKALANI
Aloha 'Oe (1891–1893)

On September 2, 1838, in the middle of the reign of Kamehameha III, Lili'u Loloku Walania Kamaka'eha was born to chiefess Keohokālole and chief Kapa'akea. In keeping with Hawaiian tradition, a hānai adoption had been arranged with high-born chief Abner Pākī and his ali'i nui wife, Konia. Earlier, the couple had given their daughter, Bernice Pauahi, to the high chiefess Kīna'u, who had already offered her sons in hānai to their uncle, Kamehameha III, thus providing the kingdom with heirs. After the adoption, Lili'u was baptized Lydia Pākī, and at the age of four she was enrolled in the missionary-run Chiefs' Children's School.

In 1862, twenty-four-year-old Lydia Pākī married John Owen Dominis, the only son of an Italian sea captain lost at sea in the 1840s. Lydia's restless intelligence, independent nature, and love of music were in stark contrast to the remote and dour man she married. While providing her with guidance in the foreigner's world, Dominis seemed an unlikely mate.

Her brother, King Kalākaua, chose her to succeed him when their brother, Leleiōhoku, died in 1877. Strong-willed and well-informed, she came to the throne prepared to rule. She believed her right to rule was God-given and in the best interests of the Hawaiian people. She watched the Bayonet Constitution, implemented in 1887, humble Kalākaua with his royal authority subordinated to a cabinet that answered to the legislature. She condemned Kalākaua's ceding of Pearl Harbor in exchange for trade advantages with the United States. Judging Kalākaua weak, Lili'uokalani opted for a more aggressive stance. Possessed of a complex personality and a regal sense of self that some considered too proud and arrogant, the new queen was not easily understood. In a time of political turmoil, her personality proved a liability, for it fed misconceptions as to her intentions that further alienated opponents already commited to ending the monarchy.

Lili'uokalani's authority as queen was vulnerable from the start, due to the declining population of her native people. In addition, economics played a significant role in undermining the monarchy. Some of the royal lands, a traditional source of wealth and authority for the crown, were surrendered during the Great Māhele of 1848. More of the land was absorbed by the government, while vast tracts, once the property of Hawaiian kings, were inherited by non-ruling ali'i. With the crown and the 'āina no longer linked, another sacred bond had been broken.

Seated left to right: Miss Laura Cleghorn, Lili'uokalani (Mrs. John O. Dominis), Princess Likelike (Mrs. Archibald S. Cleghorn), Mrs. Elizabeth Achuck (Keawepoole) Sumner. Standing: Mr. Thomas Cleghorn, Gov. John O. Dominis, Hon. Archibald S. Cleghorn, circa. 1880.

THE EARLY LIFE OF LILI'UOKALANI

Within a grass-thatched compound at the base of Punch Bowl Hill, chiefess Keohokālole prepared to give birth, attended by several ali'i, a midwife, and a kahuna to provide a priestly blessing. Through her mother, the newborn was linked to the prominent Keaweaheulu clan. Keohokālole's family had been court chanters and composers of mele, and the start of labor was accompanied by genealogical chants that told of her ancestral history and the deeds that brought her family additional mana.

Directly after her birth, the infant, named Lili'u, was wrapped in soft white kapa, the cloth made of mulberry bark, and quickly taken to the home of the high chiefess Konia, granddaughter of Kamehameha I, and her husband, the highborn chief Abner Pākī, for a pre-arranged adoption.

Several months later, the baby was christened Lydia, and wet-nursed by a lesser ali'i, a retainer in Konia's household named Kaikai. Through Kaikai, the first years of Lydia's life were spent in the spiritual embrace of old Hawai'i. At the age of four, she was enrolled in the missionary-run Chiefs' Children's School. It was here that she began an education that included a new morality. Along with her impressionable ali'i classmates, Lydia was forced to reconcile what was Hawaiian and what was foreign in attitudes, emotions, and beliefs. Although the ali'i children at the Chiefs' Children's School were trained and educated with the possibility of leading the kingdom, there seemed little likelihood that the responsibility would fall to Lydia Pākī, although time would prove otherwise. Too many others had higher claim to the throne. Lydia's musical talents seemed a more likely outlet for her energies, and she would cultivate these throughout her life, ultimately becoming one of Hawai'i's most talented composers.

As the kahuna Ka'ōpupulu had predicted a century earlier, the Hawaiians were losing claim to much of their ancestral lands.

During the spring and summer of 1891, Lili'uokalani made an extensive tour of her island kingdom. Justifiably fearing for Hawai'i's independence without the legitimacy of the monarchy, she moved to reestablish the primacy of the crown. She announced plans to draw a new constitution for the kingdom, claiming that a constitution given by a monarch such as the Bayonet Constitution under which she was named Queen, could also be revoked by royal authority. She awaited the outcome of legislative elections scheduled for 1892 that pitted newly named Liberals, in pursuit of a republic, against Reform and National Reform candidates casually supportive of the monarchy. The inconclusive outcome strengthened anti-monarchist forces.

Throughout the spring of 1892, the Liberal Party leadership continued its attacks on the government. As the tension mounted, the British navy directed a warship to Honolulu to counterbalance the presence of American warships already at anchor. Although the British remained preoccupied with other spoils of empire, they retained an interest in preserving Hawaiian independence, hoping to forestall America's expansionist ambitions.

Lili'uokalani was well aware of efforts to compromise the sovereignty of the Hawaiian Kingdom. Her more vocal opponents, led by the aggressively hostile Lorrin Thurston, and, for a time, by the quixotic part-Hawaiian, Robert Wilcox, disparaged the queen's attitude and abilities and actively espoused her overthrow. Hostile political factions, calling for revolution, began to openly surface: the Patriotic League, a rabidly anti-royalist secret society, and the Annexationist Club, led by Lili'uokalani's political enemy, Lorrin Thurston.

The legislative session that began on May 28, 1892, the longest in Hawai'i's history, focused on the economic downturn caused by tariffs and the end of reciprocity. Credit was tight, with pay cuts at all levels of government. Anti-monarchist forces in the legislature voted no confidence to all of Lili'uokalani's cabinet appointees. Within six months the cabinet had been reformed four times. The opposition wanted to force the queen's hand. Since cabinets, chosen to mollify the opposition, had not provided Hawai'i with a stable government, Lili'uokalani decided to take the initiative. On January 13, 1893, she appointed yet another cabinet, this time with members more to her liking. The following day she officiated at an impressive ceremonial end to the legislative session. She then informed the cabinet privately of her plan to proclaim a new constitution restoring royal prerogatives. She requested their presence as confirming witnesses. In conference, without the queen in attendance, her ministers concluded that they could not support the queen in what they considered a revolutionary action. Confronted with her cabinet's refusal

Lili'uokalani through the years: (1) As a young girl of fifteen; (2) as Lydia Kamaka'eha Pākī, 1860; (3) as High Chiefess Pākī, 1866; (4) as Honorable Lydia Kamaka'eha Dominis 1870.

87 | Lydia Kamaka'eha / Lili'uokalani

THE SEEDS OF REVOLUTION

To pro-business, republican forces, the monarchy was an expensive anachronism. They wanted Hawai'i's infrastructure to be upgraded to keep pace with the needs of commerce and plantation agriculture. Because of reciprocity with the United States, sugar was now the mainstay of Hawai'i's economy. In 1891, however, reciprocity was superseded by the McKinley tariffs. Overnight, Hawaiian sugar lost its price advantage in the American market. With the business community facing disaster, many felt that waiting for constitutional change was a luxury they could no longer afford. They pushed for annexation to the United States, a move that would provide a tariff-free flow of sugar.

to legitimatize a new constitution, the frustrated queen was forced to retreat.

Events were now moving with their own momentum. The Annexationist Club organized a thirteen-member Committee of Safety with the aim of creating a provisional government to replace the monarchy. Compromise was increasingly unlikely as the royal government, without organized partisans, faltered. On January 16, American troops from the USS *Boston* landed, charged with maintaining order should the situation deteriorate further. Intimidated and uncertain, and realizing perhaps the futility of resistance, Lili'uokalani's government did nothing. The Committee of Safety proclaimed a provisional government, refusing any last-ditch efforts for a negotiation. Trying to sustain a credible position, the cabinet appealed for the support of American Minister Stevens. When no word was received, the cabinet invited members of the diplomatic corps to a conference on the afternoon of the seventeenth. Stevens was conspicuously absent. Equally discouraging was the advice of those who did attend, saying that Lili'uokalani should not resist with force. The implication was ominous, for it was now believed that Stevens had committed American troops to supporting the revolutionary government, should the royal government resort to arms. That same day, having secured several government buildings not far from the palace, including the main police station which Lili'uokalani had surrendered, Stevens recognized the rebels as the de facto government of Hawai'i, and the queen was escorted from the palace.

There is a picture of the fifty-two-year-old Lili'uokalani in a high-back chair on the front lānai of 'Iolani Palace the day she was proclaimed queen. The face is indeed resolute, the demeanor dignified and humbling. History, however, was not to fulfill her dreams or ambitions. Following her overthrow, the deposed queen resided at Washington Place, having inherited the property when her husband died in 1891.

Lili'uokalani pursued restitution via the United States government, hoping American pressure could alter the course of events. Her representatives headed to Washington, where they stated her heartfelt case before Congress and the newly elected president, Grover Cleveland. Cleveland was against annexation, considering Hawai'i a sovereign nation. Under his instructions, James H. Blount traveled to Honolulu to investigate the ramifications of events and seek accurate and comprehensive information. Blount's final report to President Cleveland in mid-October clearly stated the queen's right to the Hawaiian throne, laying the blame for the revolution on the unauthorized actions of American minister Stevens. Blount called for a reevaluation by the

Continued on page 92

REVEREND SERENO E. BISHOP

In a letter to James H. Blount, special commissioner sent to Honolulu by President Grover Cleveland, annexationist Reverend Sereno E. Bishop reveals the disrespect for Native Hawaiians inherent to the revolutionary movement:

It is constantly argued that by the annexation of Hawaii without the full consent of the Natives, the United States would be committing a robbery of their rights of sovereignty and independence...such a weak and wasted people prove by their failure to save themselves from progressive extinction, and their incapacity to help or defend the denizens of Hawaii, their consequent lack of claim to continued sovereignty...It would seem that the forty millions of property interests held by foreigners must be delivered from Native misrule.

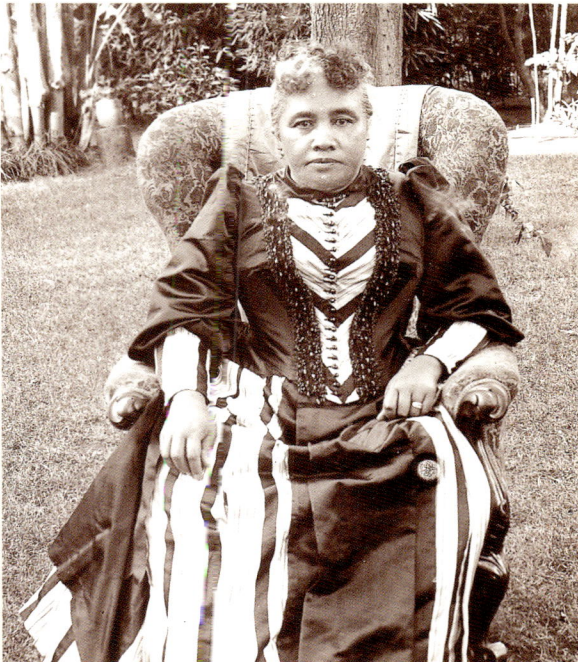

(Left) Princess Liliʻuokalani had been chosen by her brother, King Kalākaua, as his successor in 1877, following the death of their brother and heir apparent, Prince William Pitt Leleiōhoku. During King Kalākaua's lengthy tour around the world in 1881, she served as regent in his stead. (Bottom right) The deposed Queen at Washington Place, c. 1897. (Top right) John Owen Dominis, governor of Oʻahu and consort of Queen Liliʻuokalani, died in August of 1891. The couple had been childhood friends since the days when he watched Princess Lydia on the grounds of the Royal School. They were married in 1862, and lived for many years at Washington Place, the Dominis family home. Her husband's death during the first year of her reign was a great personal loss for the queen. Her reign might have evolved differently had he lived.

39 | Lydia Kamakaʻeha / Liliʻuokalani

Lydia Kamaka'eha / Lili'uokalani

(Left to right) Princess Kaʻiulani, Princess Liliʻuokalani, and Princess Poʻomaikelani on a visit to the John Cummins Sugar plantation at Waimānalo, 1887.

Lydia Kamakaʻeha / Liliʻuokalani

Continued from page 88

United States government, asking whether a great wrong done to a feeble state by the authority of the United States should not be undone by restoring the "legitimate Government."

In October, the American government sent Albert S. Willis to Honolulu to relay "sincere regret" for the "reprehensible" conduct of Stevens and the improper use of naval troops. The queen was asked to rely on the justice of the United States government to undo the "flagrant wrong" done against her. In return for such American support, she was required to offer a general amnesty to participants in the insurrection. In exchange, the United States would ask the provisional government to restore the queen to her throne.

It was an unrealistic expectation, for the annexationists were not about to accept America's intervention as a mediator. The queen's supporters, however, anticipated a rapid reversal. The interview between

THE QUEEN'S CABINET

Following the cabinet's refusal to support the queen, W. D. Alexander, a scholarly observer in government service for many years, provided an appraisal of the situation:

> To judge from their conduct, the Queen's Cabinet were overawed by the unanimity and determination of the foreign community, and probably had an exaggerated idea of the force at the command of the Committee. They shrank from the responsibility of causing fruitless bloodshed, and sought a valid excuse for inaction, which they thought they found in the presence of United States troops on shore, and in the well known sympathy of the American Minister [Stevens] with the opposition.

Immediately following the overthrow, and under protest, Lili'uokalani acknowledged, "the superior force of the United States," saying she hoped, "to avoid any collision of armed forces and perhaps loss of life…until such time as the Government of the United States shall, upon the facts being presented to it, undo the action of its representatives and reinstate me in authority which I claim as the constitutional sovereign of the Hawaiian islands." Sadly, it was to prove a futile wish.

JOHN L. STEVENS

America's resident minister, John L. Stevens, who played a crucial role in the coup d'etat that brought an end to Lili'uokalani's reign, made it clear that the new queen was expected to operate within the confines of the Bayonet Constitution:

> The Minister of the United States expresses his earnest opinion that your majesty has taken firm resolution to aid in making your reign…a strictly constitutional reign. In the wish thus to accept the supreme authority of the Constitution and the Laws, Your Majesty places yourself in the exalted rank of the best Sovereigncy of the world and thus will avoid embarrassments and perplexities of countries not blessed with free and enlightened Constitutions.

EXILE RATHER THAN PUNISHMENT

The queen sought a compromise, proposing exile for those responsible for the revolution, rather than corporal punishment. As she states in her memoirs:

> I feared the lives of myself and people would be endangered and that if any clemency were shown it must be in sparing of their [Hawaiian] lives—but they [the revolutionists] must not be permitted to stay—they and their children—for I felt that if they remained they would still continue to be a disturbing element…

Lydia Kamaka'eha / Lili'uokalani

A TALENT FOR MUSIC

Queen Liliʻuokalani was a prolific composer whose songs were reproduced in sheet music sold around the world. She wrote literally hundreds of pieces, perhaps her most famous composition being "Aloha ʻOe." It was composed in 1878 by Princess Liliʻuokalani after an outing to Maunawili Ranch, the windward Oʻahu home of Edwin Boyd. On her way home over the Pali road, she looked back and saw two lovers lingering behind for one last embrace. "Aloha ʻoe, farewell to thee," she murmured to her companions, and then, humming the rest of the way back to Honolulu, she completed the classic song by the time she returned to Washington Place. However, her most haunting melody is "Prayer and Serenade," also known as "The Queen's Prayer," published as sheet music by future Honolulu Mayor John H. Wilson. Composed in 1895 during her eight-month incarceration in a single room in ʻIolani Palace, the queen asks forgiveness for those who imprisoned her.

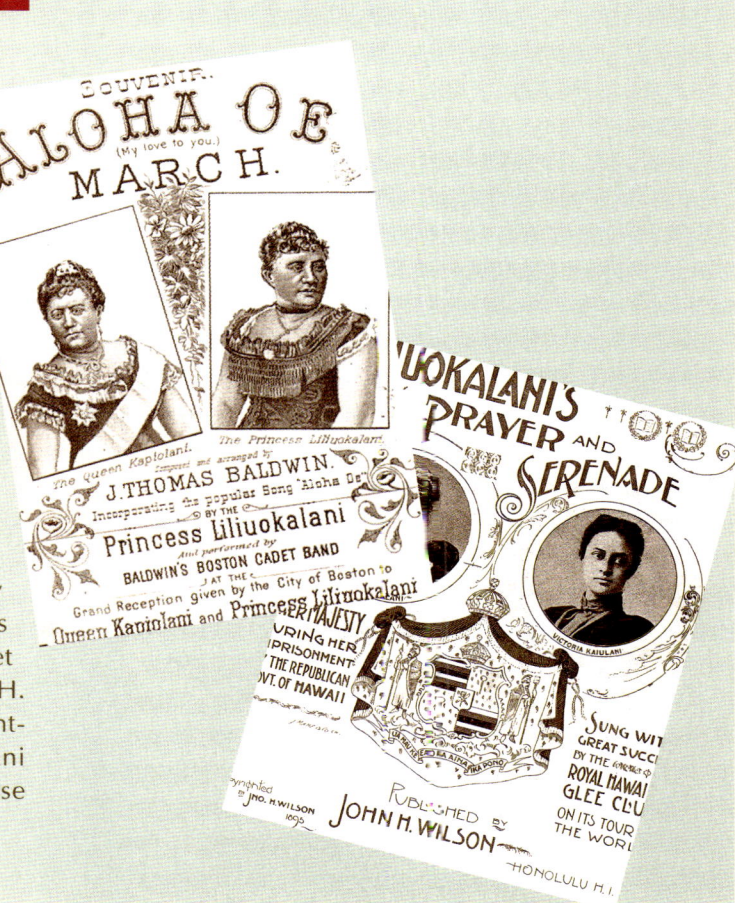

Willis and Liliʻuokalani was set for November 13. An unfortunate misunderstanding emerged from the session, with Willis reporting the queen's intention of corporal punishing those involved in the rebellion. His cable to Washington bespoke the problems that were to follow: "Views of first part [Liliʻuokalani] so extreme [the potential beheading of conspirators] as to require further instructions." Washington replied that general amnesty and recognition of the obligations of the provisional government were pre-conditions for restoration that were not open to negotiation.

Although annexation was voted down in the United States Senate, a second investigating committee drew very different conclusions than the Blount Report. Politically self-serving, it came out in favor of the provisional government. On July 4, 1894, a date chosen for obvious political benefit, the provisional government ceased to exist when the Republic of Hawaiʻi was proclaimed. Centuries of royal rule had officially ended.

A doomed counter-revolution in 1895 was led by Robert Wilcox, a member of the Republic's legislature who had returned to the royalist camp. Many claimed Liliʻuokalani was privy to plans related to an insurrection, although the evidence never went beyond circumstantial. This last effort on behalf of the monarch quickly ran its course, to be followed by new proposals for annexation in the United States Congress.

Liliʻuokalani paid a price for the attempted coup mounted on her behalf, and found herself implicated when arms were found buried on the grounds of Washington Place. Fearful of agitating the Native Hawaiian community, the government arrested the queen only after the situation was again under control. On January 16, 1895, one day short of two years following her abdication, Liliʻuokalani was taken from Washington Place and settled into a small apartment in ʻIolani Palace. Pressured by circumstances, facing trial for involvement in the counter-revolution, and demoralized by her failed efforts at restoration, on January 24 Lili'uokalani signed an abdication document renouncing her claim to the throne and proclaiming the republic the legitimate heir to the monarchy. For complicity in the ill-conceived insurgency, a military court found her guilty and imposed a $5,000 fine and five years at hard labor, a sentence that was commuted by a sympathetic President Dole. In September she was released from prison, with a full pardon approved the following year.

Free to travel, Lili'uokalani set sail for the United States, where she lectured against the overthrow, seeking to secure both popular and political support for her cause. A woman of many talents, she wrote of her life with clarity and insight in a fascinating autobiography, *Hawaii's Story by Hawaii's Queen*. On April 21, 1917, in a final compromise to the realities wrought by time, Lili'uokalani, frail at seventy-eight, walked out the front door of

January 17, 1893. The last day of delivery for the royal post office. With the unauthorized support of American Minister John Stevens, American naval troops were landed and authorized to side with the revolutionary annexationists. Lili'uokalani lost her throne and Hawai'i lost its independence.

On January 16, 1895, Queen Lili'uokalani was arrested at her Washington Place home and taken to 'Iolani Palace, where she spent over seven months under house arrest.

Lydia Kamaka'eha / Lili'uokalani

An August 2, 1898 reception at Washington Place in honor of Queen Liliʻuokalani's return from Washington, D.C. Left to right: Princess Kaʻiulani, Queen Liliʻuokalani, Prince Kūhiō, Mrs. J. O. Carter, and her daughter, Mrs. Sarah Babbit.

95 | Lydia Kamakaʻeha / Liliʻuokalani

President Dole proclaiming the Republic of Hawai'i, July 4, 1894.

Washington Place and ordered the American flag raised instead of the Hawaiian flag to commemorate those Hawaiians killed in World War I.

Lili'uokalani wrote of her feeling to her hānai daughter, Lydia K. Aholo:

> *I could not turn back the time for the political change, but there is still time to save our heritage. You must remember never to cease to act because you feel you may fail. The way to lose any earthly kingdom is to be inflexible, intolerant and prejudicial. Another way is to be too flexible, tolerant of too many wrongs, and without judgment at all. It's a razor's edge. It is the width of a blade of pili grass. To gain the kingdom of heaven is to hear what is not said, to see what cannot be seen, and to know the unknowable—that is Aloha.*

Before the year was out, Lili'uokalani was gone. At her funeral, Hawai'i's links to the royal past were acknowledged. *The Pacific Commercial Advertiser* reported the events that marked the funeral. It was a sad finale to Hawai'i's long and illustrious royal history.

> *The hundreds of watchers who had been waiting for this event, some of them for hours, saw first a procession of soldiers from the national guard, who were followed by four torch bearers, men wearing the short yellow and red capes of the chiefs of high order. Next came a group of kāhili bearers, women in black holokū and more men wearing the short capes.*
>
> *After this, immediately preceded and followed by tabu sticks that marked the limits through which none but the elect could pass, came the slow-moving hearse with its royal burden. More kāhili bearers followed, and*

Lydia Kamaka'eha / Lili'uokalani

After the overthrow of the monarchy, groups of Hawaiian supporters from all ranks of life would often gather at Washington Place, home of their deposed queen, to show support and aloha. "O ke aliʻi wale no kaʻu makemake," it was said of the love of the people for their aliʻi, "my desire is only for the chief."

immediately behind them, supported on either side by two strong men, an old, old woman in a white holokū dragged her time-tired feet, and chanted in a high, thin treble a mele telling of Her Majesty's virtues and the good that had been done by her house.

Long before midnight, in fact as early as 10 o'clock in the evening, the steps of [the] church were packed full, and the streets approaching Washington Place were lined with people, all quiet, all solemnly waiting, a silence that was almost oppressive, the passing of the last of Hawaiʻi's queens from her last home.

The long vigil, which is broken into two-hour watches, is physically very trying, as no word nor smile must pass between the watchers, and no movement is allowed of any part of their body, except the arms, as the kāhilis are kept in motion. Except for chants or wailing, the silence is never broken. ∎

An elderly Liliʻuokalani with her hānai sons, Kaipo Aea (left) and John ʻAimoku Dominis. John ʻAimoku was born in 1883, son of John Owen Dominis and Mrs. Lamiki ʻAimoku, a retainer in Liliʻuokalani's household. He was raised in Liliʻuokalani's home and was officially adopted by her in 1910. Liliʻuokalani also made Lydia Aholo her hānai daughter.

97 | Lydia Kamakaʻeha / Liliʻuokalani

November 11, 1917. Lili'uokalani's body lies in state in Kawaiaha'o Church, attended by loyal supporters, kāhili in hand.

Lydia Kamaka'eha / Lili'uokalani | 98

Lydia Kamaka'eha / Lili'uokalani

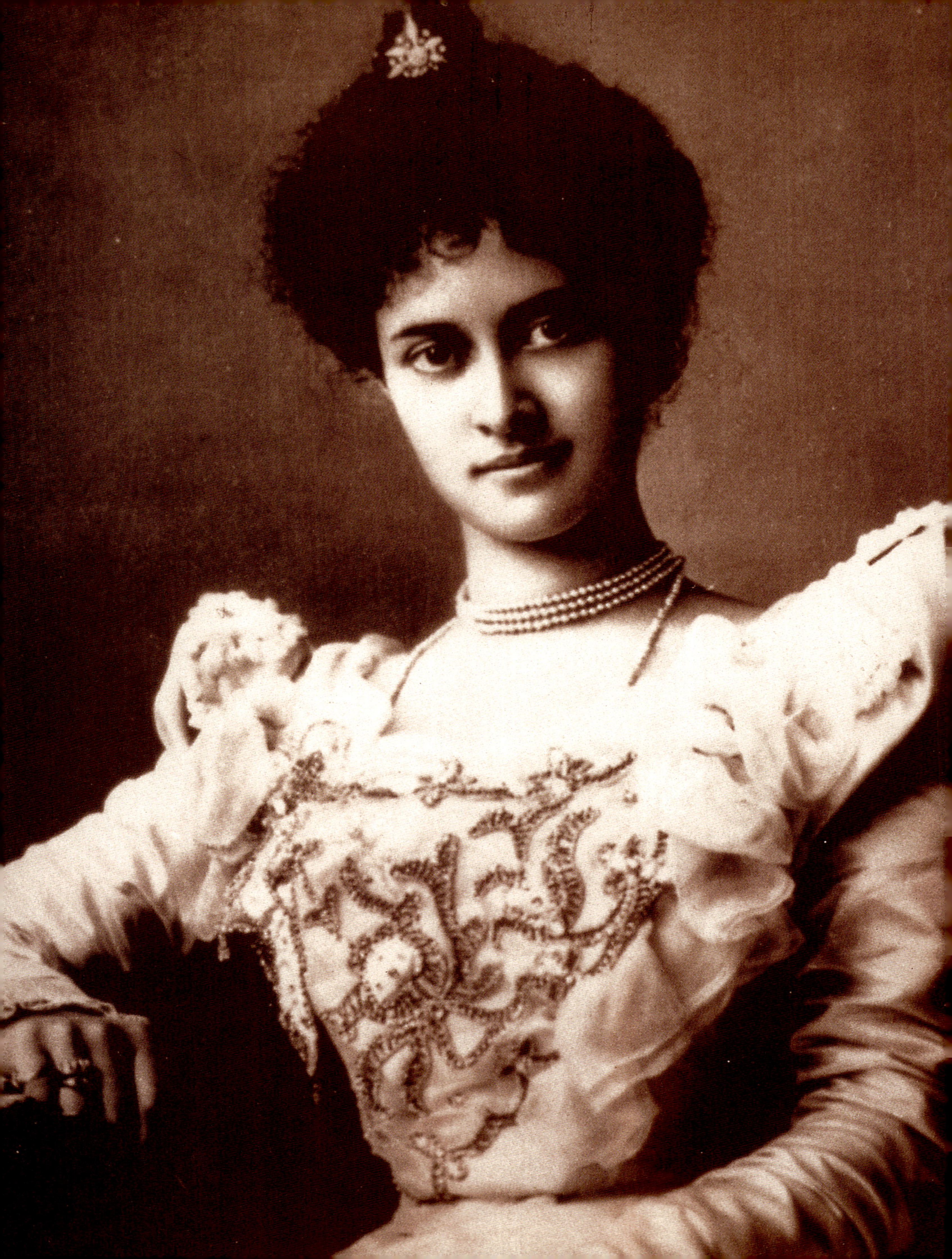

CHAPTER 13

⋆ VICTORIA KA'IULANI ⋆
The Victorian Princess (1875–1899)

Daughter of Lili'uokalani's younger sister, Miriam Likelike, Ka'iulani was born October 16, 1875, one year after Kalākaua was elected to the throne. Ka'iulani was treasured from the start, both for her beauty and for what she represented as the sole royal offspring of her generation. The blood of two peoples ran through Ka'iulani's veins: Hawaiian ali'i on her mother's side, and Scottish from her father, Archibald Cleghorn.

Ka'iulani was born one year into their marriage, and inherited her royal title at birth. Her lineage linked her to the House of Keawe. She was a great-great-great-granddaughter of Kamehameha's father, Keōua Kupuapaikalaninui, and his wife Kame'eiamoku. Ka'iulani's credentials were further strengthened when Ruth Ke'elikōlani, heiress of the Kamehamehas, was named godmother to the newborn princess. She brought a sense of the Hawaiian past into Ka'iulani's life.

In her first three years, Ka'iulani lived with her parents on Queen Emma Street not far from 'Iolani Palace. In 1878, the family moved to a ten-acre country-Victorian estate called 'Āinahau (cool place) in Waikīkī, built on land given to Ka'iulani at birth by Princess Ruth. Here Ka'iulani spent most of her childhood, becoming proficient at horseback riding, swimming, and surfing. Leading a sheltered childhood, she was confronted by tragic realities early in life, starting with the loss of Princess Ruth in 1883, when Ka'iulani was eight years old. That was followed by the sudden death of her mother three years later.

In the years to come, Ka'iulani's older half-sister, Annie Cleghorn, played a companion's role, supplementing the attention paid by the princess's father and her young English governess, Gertrude Gardinier.

By nature somewhat withdrawn, Ka'iulani nonetheless made lasting friendships from the flow of guests welcomed at 'Āinahau. British writer Robert Louis Stevenson, befriended by King Kalākaua, spent many hours with Ka'iulani. Sharing time with her at 'Āinahau, he penned sweet lines about the impressionable princess, captivated, as were many, by her innocent, melancholy spirit.

Delicate in temperament and body, refined, introspective, and possessed of intelligence and integrity, Ka'iulani was custom-made for the romantic Victorian Age into which she was born. As highest-born ali'i of her generation, she was destined for Hawai'i's throne. With Likelike's death in 1887, Ka'iulani was made second in line to succeed Kalākaua, behind her aunt Lili'uokalani. She was sent to boarding school in Europe, to be groomed for her future responsibilities as queen.

Exotic birds and plants added a distinctive touch to Ka'iulani's home in Waikīkī. Called 'Āinahau, it was located where the Princess Ka'iulani and Hyatt Regency Waikiki hotels now stand. Peacocks (pīkake) roamed the landscaped grounds, where sweet-smelling jasmine, recently introduced from India, was liberally planted. Favored by the princess, these delicate flowers were named pīkake, after her beloved peacocks.

On Friday, May 10, 1888, Ka'iulani set sail for San Francisco aboard the USS *Umatilla* to the strains of *Hawai'i Pono'i*. It was the first leg of a long journey that would eventually see Ka'iulani settled into the baronial beauty of Great Harrowden Hall, an English country boarding school for young ladies. Popular and lovely in high-necked Gibson Girl garb, she adjusted well to her life abroad despite recurring bouts of loneliness, occasional headaches, and colds. Unfortunately, the news from Hawai'i grew progressively more disturbing with revolutionary forces working to transform the Hawai'i she had left behind into an American territory.

When her uncle, David Kalākaua, died, Queen Lili'uokalani named the sixteen-year-old princess next in line to Hawai'i's throne.

Ka'iulani was still in school in England when the telegram arrived on January 30, 1893, telling of Lili'uokalani's overthrow. Her father had tried to save the monarchy by proposing the politically passive Ka'iulani as a royal substitute for Lili'uokalani. But the revolutionary Committee of Safety was no longer interested in compromise, and the proposal was politely but firmly rejected by an uncharacteristically pleasant Lorrin Thurston:

Three childhood poses of the young Princess Ka'iulani before she was sent off at thirteen for study abroad. While still at home in Hawai'i, she and her governess Gertrude Gardinier—after a somewhat rocky beginning—developed a strong and loving relationship. of Ka'iulani, Gardinier said, "She is the fragile, *spirituelle* type, but very vivacious, with beautiful large expressive dark eyes. She proves affectionate, high-spirited, at times quite willful, though usually reasonable and very impulsive and generous.

A TRIBUTE TO A PRINCESS

Robert Louis Stevenson honored Ka'iulani with this short poem when she departed for England:

*Forth from her land to mine she goes,
the Island maid, the Island rose,
Light of heart and bright of face,
The daughter of a double race.
Her Islands here in southern sun
Shall mourn their Ka'iulani,
And I, in dear banyan's shade,
Look vainly for the little maid.
But Scots Islands far away
Shall glitter with unwonted day,
And cast for once their tempest by
To smile in Ka'iulani's eye.*

Victoria Ka'iulani | 102

You know my regard for Princess Ka'iulani. I think very highly of her...but matters have proceeded too far for your plan to be an adequate answer to the situation. We are going to abrogate the monarchy entirely.

Lili'uokalani wrote Ka'iulani in May 1893, requesting that she refuse proposals that might place her on the throne:

I would simply like to add and say that should anyone write or propose or make any proposition to you in any way in regard to taking the Throne, I hope you will be guarded in your answer. The people all over the islands have petitioned to have me restored and it would make you appear in an awkward light to accept any overtures...

Ka'iulani responded quickly to her aunt's letter, emphatically reassuring her of continued loyalty, telling her of the impact of events on her health:

I have never received any proposal from anybody to take the Throne. I have not received a word of any sort from anyone except my father. I am glad to be able to say that I have not written to anyone about politics...I have considered the four years that I have been in England as years of exile. Now it seems as though things would never settle and I am simply longing to see you all— People little know how hard it is to wait patiently for news from home...I am happy as I can possibly be under the circumstances. I am really and truly recruiting my health which has not been good lately.

Fearful of self-reproach and mindful of the responsibilities of her ali'i status, Ka'iulani left London for the United States to plead for a restoration of the monarchy. She was welcomed in New

(Right) At sixteen, a young Archibald Cleghorn—of Scotland by way of New Zealand—arrived in Honolulu with his family. His father, a landscape architect, came hoping to work for the kingdom in that capacity. When the job didn't materialize, he established a dry goods store which young Cleghorn took over when his father died two years later. Archibald had a good head for business. The business prospered; and in four years he had stores on several Islands. In 1870, at 35, he married ali'i Miriam Likelike, seventeen years his junior.

Ka'iulani's mother, Miriam Likelike was made a princess when her brother, David Kalākaua, ascended the throne in 1874. She died when Ka'iulani was only twelve years old. Her death was a disheartening loss, willed to death—some believed—by a hostile kahuna 'ana'ana, a practitioner of the old religion. Shyest of the Kalākaua royals, Likelike seemed an unlikely victim of such hostile forces. Others said that Likelike surrendered to a self-imposed belief that her death was required to placate the goddess Pele, whose molten lava was again threatening Hilo. Still others claimed her death followed complications following a miscarriage. It is also said that on her deathbed, Likelike told Ka'iulani that she would leave Hawai'i for a long time, never to marry or reign as queen. The startled princess had run from the room crying.

103 | Victoria Ka'iulani

York, Boston, and Washington, where she was received by President Grover Cleveland. Her intelligence and exotic beauty helped move President Cleveland to send James Blount to Honolulu to recommend a course of action for the American government concerning restoration of the monarchy. With events in Hawai'i unsettled, her father resisted her wish to return to the Islands. Ka'iulani instead returned to Great Harrowden Hall, where in the isolation of the English countryside, her education continued.

Whatever the American decision, unseating the Republican government and restoring the monarchy would prove no easy task. Lili'uokalani wrote from Honolulu describing the uncertainties of the situation. She proposed marriage for Ka'iulani, suggesting either her cousin, David Kawānanakoa, or perhaps a Japanese prince, thereby involving Japan in the desperate effort to maintain Hawai'i's independence. Ka'iulani responded with a hope that her marriage would be based on love rather than political expediency, although she was ready to acquiesce, should her aunt consider it an absolute necessity. The provisional government, with no intention of surrendering the power it had usurped, created the Republic of Hawai'i with an aim of eventual annexation by the United States, where a new president, William McKinley, was about to be inaugurated. With each passing month, hopes for a restoration dimmed. Lili'uokalani's arrest and incarceration added to her sense of helplessness and isolation. Sensing the outcome in final balance, Ka'iulani begged her father to let her return to Hawai'i. He acquiesced, and a rendezvous was set, again in Washington, D.C., where Lili'uokalani and Cleghorn were headed to plead the royal case with President McKinley. Although the reunion with her family was a happy one, the outcome of their efforts would not prove so satisfactory.

THE HOPES AND DREAMS OF A NATION

Lili'uokalani later wrote in her memoirs of the hopes her niece inspired, providing the promise of a future for the Kalākaua dynasty: "Princess Likelike brought boundless joy to the family and the nation by giving birth to a daughter. The hopes of all centered on this baby, Princess Ka'iulani.

Even with Ka'iulani's attempts to gain support for the monarchy, the United States Congress voted for annexation, and on August 12, 1898, Hawai'i officially became an American territory. The future seemed uncertain for Ka'iulani when she headed to the island of Hawai'i for the wedding of her friend Eva Parker. Disillusioned by life in Americanized Honolulu, saddened by the injustice of circumstance, she expressed in a letter to Lili'uokalani, written as 1898 drew to a close, feelings alive in most Hawaiian hearts.

They have taken away everything from us and it seems there is left but a little, and that little our very life itself. We live now in such a semi retired way, that people wonder if we even exist any more. I wonder too, and to what purpose?

Caught in a rainstorm while horseback riding in the hills above Waimea on the Big Island, she contracted a fever. Cleghorn, fearing for his daughter's health, headed for the Big Island accompanied by the family doctor. Within several weeks she seemed well enough to return to Honolulu. Bedridden, Ka'iulani lingered for two months. Then, at 2 a.m., on March 6, 1899, Victoria Ka'iulani, the princess of Hawai'i's heart, died at age twenty-three. ■

When, in 1897, Ka'iulani returned to Hawai'i and her Waikīkī home 'Āinahau, it was as heir presumptive to a non-existent throne. She expressed her dismay in a letter to Lili'uokalani: "Last Sunday the Hawaiians came out to see me. There were several hundred, and by six o'clock I didn't know what to do with myself. I was so tired. It made me feel so sad to see so many of the Hawaiians looking so poor. In the old days I am sure there were not so many people almost destitute..." Distraught and with her life forever changed, became ill and died Mrach 6, 1899, deeply mourned, at age twenty-three.

Ka'iulani (right) feeds a peacock while talking with her half-sister, Annie Cleghorn, who sits next to her on the steps at 'Āinahau. Cousin David Kawānanakoa (left) is paying a visit, circa 1898.

105 | Victoria Ka'iulani

"Animated, capricious, headstrong, yes, but her vivacity had a certain quiet sadness. Her eyes were too large above cheeks flushed hectically; but such pride of bearing, love of companions and heartfelt loyalty of feeling for her native Hawaiians." Thus a contemporary described Princess Kaʻiulani in the mid-1890s. Kaʻiulani spent her childhood at the family's Waikīkī estate, ʻĀinahau. Groomed as heir apparent to the throne, she would have succeeded Liliʻuokalani, but the Hawaiian monarchy ended with its first and last queen.

(Above) In 1889, Princess Kaʻiulani posed in a Japanese kimono shortly before leaving the Islands to go to school in England.

(Left) Princess Kaʻiulani sits with her croquet partners beneath her banyan tree at ʻĀinahau. Her half-sister, Anne, is seated in front.

Victoria Kaʻiulani

Following the official raising of the American flag over ʻIolani Palace on August 12, 1898, a commission was sent to the Hawaiian Islands to assess the situation. Throughout the commissioners' travels of the Islands, formal petitions against annexation were presented by Native Hawaiians, including during dinners or gatherings. On the evening of October 1, 1898, Princess Kaʻiulani gave a glittering banquet and ball at her ʻĀinahau home in Waikīkī as part of an effort by loyalists to the Hawaiian Kingdom to reverse annexation.

Victoria Kaʻiulani

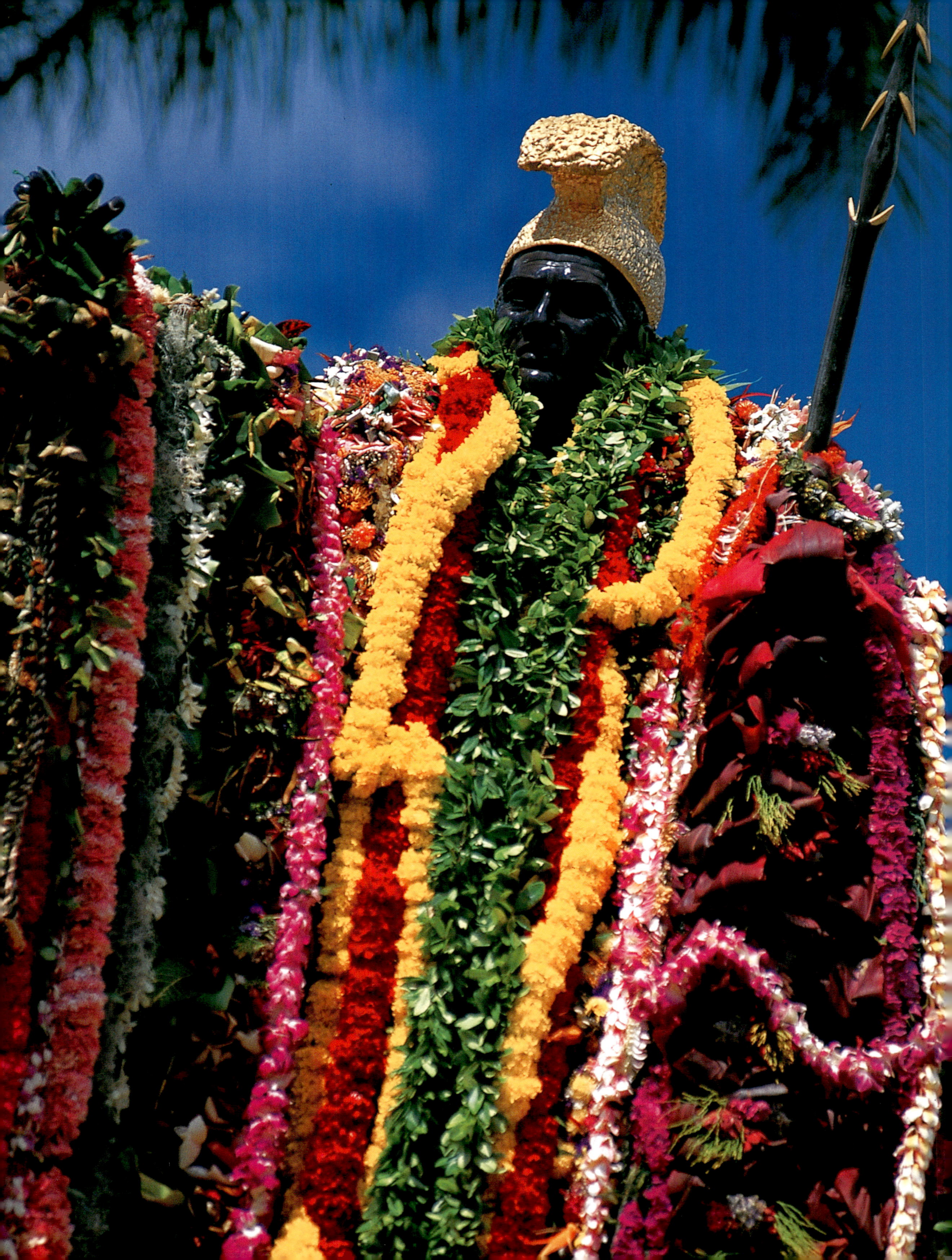

CHAPTER 14

THE ALI‘I LEGACY

More than a century since the last ali‘i ruled, and death brought an end to one noble line after another, the royal lands of Hawai‘i have been inherited by the Hawaiian people. Along with a history rich in intriguing detail and an inspiring idealized role model, it is these lands, a spiritual as well as a physical resource, that are the most important ali‘i legacy. In the last few decades of the nineteenth century, four ali‘i created trusts to serve the well-being of their people in perpetuity.

King Lunalilo focused his attention on the old, while Bernice Pauahi made education her cause. Queen Lili‘uokalani left her estate to fund a range of social services for Hawaiian children. The resources of Queen Emma's substantial estate was committed to health care at a time when diseases and infertility were pushing the Hawaiians to extinction. Queen Kapi‘olani, while not establishing a trust, founded and funded a hospital that bears her name, along with the beautiful park at the foot of Diamond Head, donated to the people of Hawai‘i in 1877 by her husband, King Kalākaua. These legacies established by royal grant are an integral part of contemporary Hawai‘i, a credit to the hopes of their benefactors and the efforts of those whose commitment of time and aloha give substance to this ali‘i legacy.

THE LUNALILO HOME

When William Charles Lunalilo died in 1873, his estate consisted of thirty-five parcels of land on the five main islands, totaling several thousand acres. The terms of his will called for the creation of the Lunalilo Trust to provide for his father, ali‘i Charles Kana‘ina. Upon Kana‘ina's death in 1877, with additional financial help from King Kalākaua and the

(Opposite) The gilded bronze statue of Kamehameha I decked in birthday lei. Kamehameha still provides Hawaiian history with a sense of focus and pride.

The first Lunalilo Home opened in 1883 on thirty acres on the slopes of still-rural Punchbowl Crater.

government, the trust established a home for poor and infirm Hawaiians in Lunalilo's large, Victorian-style mansion in Moanalua. By the 1920s, after more than forty years of use, the building had fallen into disrepair. In 1927 the home was moved to a new twenty-acre site in the remote flatlands at the foot of Koko Crater. The land was paid for by a $40,000 donation from the family of businessman "Cabby" Brown and his ali‘i-descended wife, Irene I‘i. A new Lunalilo Home opened a short time later. Today, a modest $2 million endowment provides full care for seniors of Hawaiian or part-Hawaiian blood, most of whom are in their eighties and nineties, many assisted by subsidies. Having sold most of its landholdings to finance operations, the only royal trust to so diminish its most valued assets, the Trust remains financially vulnerable.

THE QUEEN'S MEDICAL CENTER

In a speech to the legislature, Kamehameha IV first made note of the "decrease of our population...a subject, in comparison with which all others sink into insignificance." The king followed this observation by making public health part of his government's agenda. Within a year, a Board of Health was created and staffed, and the minister of the interior was authorized to establish hospitals on each of the major islands "for the sick poor, being natives of this kingdom." Efforts to fund these hospitals floundered for two years. But, in 1859, his wife, Queen Emma, made the establishment of a hospital a personal crusade. With a goal of $5,000 (the government had committed to supplying land when this amount had been collected), Emma and Kamehameha IV headed to the streets, notebooks in hand, soliciting contributions. Within several days the royal couple had received pledges of $14,000, to open Queen's Hospital, named in Emma's honor, at a site called Manamana, or place of "much spiritual power."

When she died in 1885, Queen Emma's will called for the creation of the Queen Emma Foundation, committing its resources to the support of the hospital she helped found. The Foundation now provides a multi-million dollar contribution to the Queen's Medical Center each year, to cover a yearly tab for charity and community-benefit medical services of more than $30 million. Today, the Queen's Medical Center pursues state-of-the-art medicine, still committed to the vision and compassion of its founding ali'i.

QUEEN LILI'UOKALANI'S CHILDREN CENTER

When Lili'uokalani died in 1917 at the age of seventy-nine, $125,000 from her estate was used to create the Lili'uokalani Trust to secure foster homes and provide necessary follow-up services. In 1948 an autonomous agency was established, and in 1966 an actual social service center was opened. Today, the Trust operates regional divisions, with outreach centers on O'ahu, the Island of Hawai'i, Maui, Kaua'i, Moloka'i, and Lāna'i. Most of the services provided are in the home, with professionally trained staffers assisted by kupuna or elders well-versed in Hawaiian culture. Participation by kupuna plays a crucial role, introducing Hawaiian culture and belief to many people who have lost touch with their roots. The center remains focused on "strengthening families, enabling them to provide safe, nurturing, permanent homes for their children." Funds are

(Left) The Queen's Hospital opened in 1864, through the efforts of Queen Emma and Kamehameha IV who personally solicited funds for its construction.

(Right) The Queen's Medical Center in the late 20th century.

The Ali'i Legacy

Keoni Sandal, with his wife Clarissa and daughter Kaitlin. In need of help at the age of 15, when his father died, Keoni turned to the Queen Liliʻuokalani Children's Center, an organization funded by the Queen Liliʻuokalani Trust to help orphaned and destitute Hawaiian children. Thousands of Hawaiian children have benefited from the trust since its founding in 1909. Funded by revenues generated by trust lands in Waikīkī and on the Island of Hawaiʻi, it continues to serve Native Hawaiian children throughout the Islands.

generated from land holdings that include acreage in the heart of Waikīkī.

THE KAMEHAMEHA SCHOOLS

On October 31, 1883, Bernice Pauahi, last of the royal Kamehamehas and heiress to tens of thousands of acres spread throughout the Islands, affixed her signature to a will that committed almost all of her vast estate to the establishment of two schools for the benefit of native Hawaiians. Today, with holdings valued at billions of dollars, the Kamehameha Schools are the best endowed secondary school in the United States.

Thirty-seven students and four teachers made up the first class of the newly formed Kamehameha School for Boys when it opened in 1887. Seven years later a school for girls opened, fulfilling the aims of Pauahi's will. Since that time, the Kamehameha Schools have grown with tens of thousands of people annually involved in its educational activities. Nurturing cultural pride, communal awareness, and self-confidence, the Kamehameha Schools remain committed to the disciplined standards that guided Pauahi throughout her life.

I desire my trustees to provide first and chiefly a good education in the common English branches, and also instruction in morals and in such useful knowledge as may tend to make good and industrious men and women.

Matters of admission, fees, curriculum, and educational focus were left to the discretion of trustees selected and confirmed by the highest court of Hawaiʻi's judicial system. While the bulk of Bishop Estate wealth remains vested in land, diversification provides the estate with substantial

The Aliʻi Legacy

Aerial view of the Kamehameha Schools' campus.

Kamehameha Schools' marching band participates in the annual Kamehameha Day Parade. The school offers extensive on- and off-campus activities that provide students with a subsidized, excellent education despite scandals that have tarnished its administrative reputation.

assets on the U.S. mainland. Revenues generated by land sales, lease payments, and investments generate hundreds of millions annually, with well over $100 million in educational expenditures at its Kapalama Heights campus and at campuses on the neighbor islands. The Estate, in its own words, remains committed to "actively and prudently managing the assets Pauahi left us." ■

The Ali'i Legacy

CHAPTER 15

THE TWENTY-FIRST CENTURY AND BEYOND

By the start of the twentieth century, Hawai'i's Native population had declined to fewer than 30,000. Family after family of ali'i died without issue, leaving the Hawaiians without the traditional guidance of a ruling class. If mana was the spiritual heritage of the ali'i, then their decline was a significant loss to Native Hawaiians. As advisors and administrators, priests and soldiers, and as both political and spiritual leaders, the ali'i played a pivotal role in Hawaiian life. They were an essential part of the cosmological balance, as fundamental to the well-being of the nation as were links to the 'āina, the land. The vacuum created by their decline was filled by the foreigners who had transformed Hawai'i into an American territory.

While Lili'uokalani lived until 1917, almost all the other nineteenth-century royals passed on before the new century began. The few ali'i coming of age as the twentieth century dawned, were a generation whose links to the old traditions were diluted by cultural assimilation. However, many Hawaiians retained a traditional respect, admiration, and loyalty toward those ali'i who survived. In the elections of 1900, when Hawai'i chose a representative to serve as a liaison between the Islands and the United States, all three contenders had ali'i blood, although each represented a different political perspective. Radical reformer Robert Wilcox was elected in 1900, serving until 1902, when Queen Kapi'olani's nephew, Prince Jonah Kūhiō Kalaniana'ole, was elected to the first of ten two-year terms. His name, which means "the royal chief without measure," clearly defined him as a traditional Hawaiian.

As hereditary kahuna nui of the Mo'okini Luakini heiau, Leimomi Mo'okini Lum helps reconcile ancient tradition and modern belief. She traces her descent to priestly ancestors who reached the Island of Hawai'i at the start of the ninth century and built the first temple at Mo'okini. Kamehameha was born within sight of the heiau, where he was taken for his birth rites. Momi officiates at ceremonies and prayers as dusk descends on Mo'okini.

PRINCE JONAH KŪHIŌ KALANAIANA'OLE

Jonah Kūhiō Kalaniana'ole and his brothers, Edward and David Kawānanakoa, were sons of Queen Kapi'olani's sister, Kinoiki Kekaulike, and chief David Kahalepouli Pi'ikoi. While not much is known of their father's genealogy, through their mother, they were descended from Kaua'i's last king, Kekaulike. Their mother's status was well-recognized and she served as governor of the Island of Hawai'i during Kalākaua's reign.

In order to assure continuity of his dynasty, Kalākaua adopted David and Jonah, making them royal princes in line to the throne after Lili'uokalani. They carried the royal crowns at Kalākaua's coronation in 1883.

Jonah Kūhiō Kalaniana'ole spent many years of his life away from Hawai'i, being educated in California and England. When he returned home in 1896, he married the full-blooded Kaua'i chiefess Elizabeth Kahanu Ka'auwai. The union unfortunately produced no children. Kūhiō's chances of ascending to the throne were shattered by the overthrow of the monarchy in 1893. Two years later, Kūhiō, affectionately called Prince Cupid for a childhood resemblance to the cherubic messenger of love, was arrested for treason in the failed counter-revolution by royalist forces. Charges were lodged against him for failing to report the "treasonous" activities to the republic's officials. Though he pleaded not guilty, he was convicted and spent the next year as a political prisoner. After his release, seeming to accept the overthrow as irreversible, he came to view annexation by the United States as preferable to the republic. In 1902, two years after Hawai'i became a territory of the United States, Kūhiō, now a Republican Party stalwart, was elected the Hawaiian representative to the United States Congress.

The nearly twenty years Kūhiō served in Washington helped generate considerable sympathy and support for Hawaiian causes. The most significant outcome of his efforts was the creation of the Hawaiian Homes Commission in 1921. Designed to provide Native Hawaiians with lands for homesteading, the Hawaiian Homes Commission remains committed to a goal it has sadly failed to achieve. Kūhiō explained the position of Native Hawaiians with stirring eloquence. In a speech before the Congress, he spoke of the decline of his people, who numbered fewer than 24,000 in the 1920 census: "The Hawaiian race is passing. And if conditions continue to exist as they do today, this splendid race of people, my people, will pass from the face of the earth... The legislation proposed seeks to place the Hawaiian back on the soil, so that the valuable and sturdy traits of that race, peculiarly adapted to the islands, shall be preserved to posterity."

In 1919, Kūhiō, well-liked, well-known, and sincerely respected in Hawai'i and Washington, sponsored a bill calling for Hawaiian statehood a full forty years before it became a reality. America, in an isolationist mood after World War I, was not interested in absorbing its exotic, mid-Pacific territory. In Hawai'i, Kūhiō organized a number of civic and honorary societies.

Kūhiō died in Honolulu in 1922 at the age of fifty and was given the last state funeral held in Hawai'i for an ali'i. After a week of ceremonial mourning, he was buried in the Royal Mausoleum in Nu'uanu Valley on O'ahu.

The Pi'ikoi brothers: Jonah Kūhiō Kalaniana'ole (standing, left), David Kawānanakoa (standing, right), and Edward Abner Keli'iahonui, dressed in student uniforms, c. 1880. Edward, eldest of the three, died while still an unmarried youth.

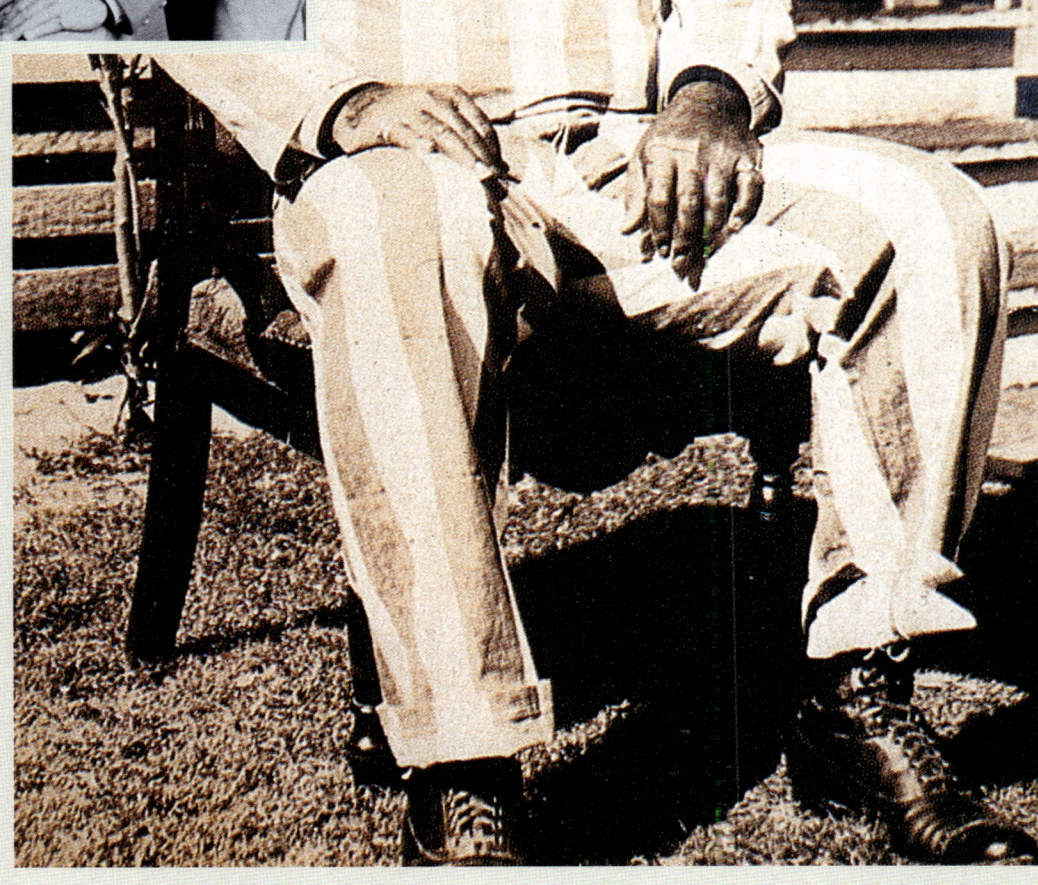

Dressed in prison garb for his participation in the counterrevolution of 1895, Prince Jonah Kūhiō Kalaniana'ole played a significant role representing Hawai'i in Washington after annexation was a fait accompli.

115 | The Twenty-First Century and Beyond

DAVID KAWĀNANAKOA

Kūhiō's older brother, David Kawānanakoa, born in 1868, was schooled outside of Hawai'i, primarily in California and England. Handsome, self-confident, and sophisticated, he and his brother visited many royal courts during their European sojourn. Returning to Hawai'i, Kawānanakoa took a position with the royal government, serving in the Ministry of Foreign Affairs. In the counter-revolution of 1895, Kawānanakoa remained on the sidelines. One of 200 people arrested by the government when the insurgency was suppressed, he was released within hours. In 1900, the thirty-two-year-old prince pursued the position his brother would gain two years later, running as a Democrat for Hawai'i's delegate to the United States Congress. The Republicans fielded the more conservative Colonel Sam Parker, an ali'i from the Island of Hawai'i. The victory went to Robert Wilcox, a populist third-party candidate who ran under the Home Rule banner. Defeated, Kawānanakoa withdrew from frontline electoral politics, preferring to operate behind the scenes as leader of the Democratic Party, a position he held until his death in 1908 at the age of forty. Although Kawānanakoa died young, he shared six years of marriage with Abigail Wahiika'ahu'ula Campbell, daughter of sugar millionaire and real estate investor, James Campbell, and ali'i Abigail Kuaihelani Ma'ipinepine. It was a fortuitous union, providing the Kawānanakoas with wealth to match their prestige, and, through their children, a new generation of ali'i to maintain the family line and links to Hawai'i's royal past.

Prince David Kawānanakoa at the turn of the 20th century. His offspring are heirs to ali'i status and the wealth of the Campbell Estate.

TODAY'S ROYALS

Today the royal family is represented by the children and grandchildren of David and Abigail's two daughters, Abigail Kapi'olani and Lydia Lili'uokalani. Some bear the family name Kawānanakoa, others bear the name Marignoli.

Softspoken and unassuming, Edward Kawānanakoa, Abigail's first cousin, was considered by many as the ali'i who would be king if Hawai'i was still a monarchy. His mana, derived from both parental lines, is well documented with links to the same ancestral stock as the Kamehamehas. There are other royal claimants. Owana Ka'ohelelani Salazar bases her claims of descent on Kaua'i's ruling chiefs through her great-grandmother, Princess Theresa Ka'ohelelani.

OTHER ALI'I

Through genealogical roots of family tradition ancestry is traced back to ali'i roots. The degree to which intermarriage has altered the Polynesian is indicated by names like Wilcox, Boyd, Brandt, Wong, Topolinski, and Smart.

The complex web of marriages that marked Polynesian Hawai'i, with most ali'i taking more than one husband or wife, saw family trees grow with intricate differentiations of status among people closely related by blood. With nearly two centuries now separating Hawaiians from the genealogical certainty of pre-contact times, centuries when the main branches of ali'i families died off, royal lineages are difficult to track and verify.

Today, traditional Hawaiian values and culture are revitalized as Native Hawaiians seek some degree of sovereignty. It remains to be seen what role ali'i will play in this rebirth of Hawaiian consciousness, for ali'i status no longer carries with it inherent privileges or responsibilities. The future will depend on the course of the current Hawaiian sovereignty movement and the outcome of the struggle to attain some degree of autonomy. If there was a certain inevitability to the end of the monarchical century and the loss of Hawaiian independence, it is equally inevitable that history never stands still for long. Hawai'i may be at one of those pivotal moments where change is again in the offing and history is being made. With some degree of sovereignty a goal of many Hawaiians, the ali'i concept and the monarchy it spawned remain a potential source of pride, inspiration, and unity. Both those who lay claim to ali'i descent and those who speak on behalf of the Hawaiian people will need to maintain the integrity of those ideals, restoring a historic bond between a people and their culture. ∎

(Left, top) Abigail Campbell Kawānanakoa, daughter of David and Elizabeth Kawānanakoa, hosted Edward, the Prince of Wales, when he visited Hawai'i in 1920. Links between the British crown and the Hawaiian monarchy began during the days of Cook and Vancouver.

(Left, middle) Abigail Kinoiki Kekaulike Kawānanakoa and her cousin Edward Kawānanakoa make a presentation of Kalākaua-era royal silver to 'Iolani Palace, c. 1980. Related to Queen Kapi'olani, both are ali'i of high rank. Some claim Edward's genealogy would have placed him on Hawai'i's throne had the monarchy survived.

(Left, bottom) Abigail Kinoiki Kekaulike with Regina Keōpūolani Kawānanakoa and Andrew Pi'ikoi Kawānanakoa, two of the five children of her cousin Edward. Circa 1975. In addition to several first cousins, they carry the Kawānanakoa line into the twenty-first century.

(Below) Owana Ka'ohelelani Salazar claims ali'i descent through her great grandmother's links to Kauai'i's ruling chiefs.

112 | The Twenty-First Century and Beyond

(Above) 1992. A proclamation announces a monarchy restored by one of several claimants to Hawai'i's empty throne.

(Inset) March 18, 1959. The *Star-Bulletin* headline story tells of the successful efforts of Lorrin P. Thurston, chairman of the Hawai'i Statehood Commission. He was the son of Lorrin A. Thurston, prominent leader in the overthrow of the monarchy.

The Twenty-First Century and Beyond | 118

(Above) During Onipaʻa, the centennial observance of the overthrow of the Hawaiian monarchy, which ended the reign of Queen Liliʻuokalani, lei draped the Queen's statue located between ʻIolani Palace and the Hawaiʻi State Capitol.

(Right) A replica of Queen Liliʻuokalani's royal standard, a symbol of Liliʻuokalani's lasting impact instilling Hawaiian pride, was displayed during Onipaʻa.

119 | The Twenty-First Century and Beyond

During Onipa'a, the 'Ahahui Ka'ahumanu in their traditional black holokū and feather lei 'ilima gathered at Mauna 'Ala, Hawai'i's Royal Mausoleum.

During Onipa'a, Hawai'i's royal organizations proudly participated in the events marking the centennial overthrow of the Kingdom of Hawai'i. (Above, left) The Royal Order of Kamehameha entered Mauna 'Ala, the Royal Mausoleum in Nu'uanu Valley. (Above, right) The royal societies pay homage at the tomb of the Kalākaua Dynasty.

The Twenty-First Century and Beyond

Carrying pūloʻuloʻu that announce the presence of aliʻi, a processional makes its way from the Puʻukoholā Heiau at a reconciliation ceremony at the sacred site.

121 | The Twenty-First Century and Beyond

Chronology of Important Events

1778—January 18, accidental arrival in Hawaiian waters of English explorer James Cook, who sights Island of O'ahu, Kaua'i, and Ni'ihau (as well as islets Lehua and Kaula, off Ni'ihau) on his way to far north Arctic Sea in search of a navigable passage from the Pacific to the Atlantic—effectively accomplishing for the western world, the discovery of an archipelago discovered and populated by Polynesians hundreds of years earlier. His ships *Resolution* and *Discovery* anchor off Kaua'i and Ni'ihau; visit villages, trade, and fraternize with natives before departing February 2, to resume search for a northwest passage.

—Finding no such passage, Cook returns to winter in the Islands he named Sandwich Islands in honor of his patron, the Earl of Sandwich, First Lord of the Admiralty, where he sites the Island of Maui (November 26) and Moloka'i and a few days later Hawai'i.

1779—Capt. Cook slain in a melee at Ka'awaloa, Kealakekua Bay (February 14).

1782—Kalani'ōpu'u, king of the Island of Hawai'i, dies (April), leaving his kingdom to his son Kīwala'ō, but entrusts the feathered image Kūkā'ilimoku, the war god of the kings of Hawai'i Island, to his nephew Kamehameha. Civil war ensues.

—Battle of Moku'ōhai, between Kamehameha and Kīwala'ō at Keomo, Hawai'i, in which Kamehameha triumphs; Kīwala'ō is slain by Ke'eaumoku; and the Island of Hawai'i is divided among three ruling chiefs—Kamehameha, Keoua, and Kewaema'uhili (July).

1786-1787—British Captains Nathaniel Portlock and George Dixon, with the ships *King George* and *Queen Charlotte,* on trading voyages between west coast of America and China, make three visits to Islands of Hawai'i for reprovisioning and scientific recording (May-June '86; Nov. '86; Sept. '87).

1788—Kamehameha I first acquires firearms; so does Kahekili, high chief on Maui.

1790—American brig *Eleanora* visits the Islands; Simon Metcalf, master, orders the Olowalu Massacre, provoking Hawaiians to retaliate, which they accomplish by capturing the *Eleanora's* tender, the *Fair American,* killing all the crew except Issac Davis who is captured. The *Eleanora's* boatswain, John Young, also captured; and both men become advisors to Kamehameha.

—Kamehameha invades Maui and wages fierce battle with Kalanikūpule in mountain passes near Wailuku, utilizing guns and cannon. Corpses of the slain are so numerous they choke up waters of 'Iao Valley stream, causing the battle to be called Kapaniwai—the damming of the waters.

—Keawema'uhili slain by Keoua in battle at Alae, in Hilo section of Hawai'i Island.

1791—Naval battle off Waimanu, Hawai'i Island, in which Kamehameha defeats both Ka'eo, king of Kaua'i, and Kahekili, king of O'ahu. Both sides utilized western artillery. Kamehameha's forces were in double canoes fitted with mounted swivel guns and small cannon under direction of John Young and Issac Davis; the battle became known as Kepuawaha'ula'ula, the battle of the red-mouthed gun.

—Keoua is slain at Kawaihae, Hawai'i, by Ke'eaumoku, while he is landing to hold conference with Kamehameha.

—Kamehameha I becomes sole ruler of all of the island of Hawai'i.

1793—Kamehameha entertains George Vancouver, commander of the *Discovery* and the *Chatham,* with a sham battle at Hawai'i; Kamehameha presents Vancouver with feathered regalia; Vancouver lands cattle for Kamehameha. Vancouver returns in 1794 with additional cattle; Kamehameha places a kapu on the livestock that it may multiply.

1794—Aboard *Discovery,* Vancouver—as follow-up to discussions with Kamehameha in 1793—again suggests Kamehameha put Hawai'i under the protection of Great Britain; Kamehameha, interested in an alliance with the great naval power and not understanding international law, cedes Hawai'i to Great Britain; the British flag is hoisted (February 25). Although the cession was never accepted by Great Britain, this event leads to English supremacy in Hawai'i for many years.

—Kahekili, king of Maui, dies at Waikīkī, O'ahu, and is succeeded by his son Kalanikūpule. On November 21, Captain William Brown, master of the *Jackal,* enters the recently discovered harbor at Honolulu.

1795—Kamehameha subdues Maui, Lāna'i, and Moloka'i (February).

—The Battle of Nu'uanu Valley, O'ahu. Kalanikūpule is joined by Kaiana, who has seceded from Kamehameha's ranks (April). Kaiana is slain but Kalanikūpule escapes to be captured some months later and sacrificed at the Papa'ena'ena heiau at the foot of Diamond Head.

—O'ahu falls into the hands of Kamehameha, who establishes headquarters at Waikīkī beach.

1796—Kamehameha, hoping to conquer Kaua'i and Ni'ihau, embarks in a fleet of war canoes outfitted with cannon but is driven back to O'ahu by a violent wind (April).

—Nāmakehā, brother of Kaiana, rebels on the Island of Hawai'i; Kamehameha returns from O'ahu and defeats Nāmakehā, in a battle at Hilo (September); Nāmakehā, escapes but is captured several months later and is sacrificed at Kipapaloa Heiau, in Pi'ihonua, Hilo, January 1797.

—Kamehameha begins construction of peleleu canoes, a fleet of extraordinarily large war canoes—utilizing western as well as Hawaiian design elements. Deep, broad, and long, some carried as many as 100 men and were fitted with cannons.

1797—Promulgation of "Māmalahoa" ("Law of the Splintered Paddle"); this edict from Kamehameha protects old and young as they travel about.

1801—Peleleu fleet arrives at Kawaihae, Hawai'i.

1802—Peleleu fleet arrives at Lāhainā, Maui.

—Kamehameha I fails in a second attempt to take over Kaua'i.

1803—Kamehameha moves on to O'ahu with the Peleleu fleet.

1804—Determined to bring Kaua'i under his control, Kamehameha prepares a fleet to invade Kaua'i; but an epidemic—possibly cholera or typhoid—strikes O'ahu, incapacitating Kamehameha and troops; invasion is called off; Peleleu fleet never sails.

1808—Hawaiian flag is designed. Family traditions credit design to Capt. George Beckley, English navigator and military adviser to Kamehameha I.

1810—King Kaumuali'i cedes island of Kaua'i to Kamehameha I.

1815—Russians arrive at Kaua'i and commit offenses, hoisting the Russian flag.

1816—Kalanimioku begins building of fort at Honolulu; upon completion in 1817 it is commanded by Capt. George Beckley.

1819—Kamehameha the Great (I) dies at Kailua (May 8). Liholiho, approximately twenty-two, is given the title of Kamehameha II.

—Ka'ahumanu is successful in getting Kamehameha II to eat in presence of women, thus breaking significant kapu—the prohibition against men and women eating together; collapse of entire system follows, including destruction of temples and idols; this leaves kingdom striped of its state religion (October).

—High chief Kalanimoku is baptized aboard the French ship *L'Uranie.*

—Kekuaokalani, Kamehameha I's nephew and heir to war god Kuka'ilimoku, leads insurrection against breaking of kapu; both Kekuaokalani and his wife are killed in battle at Kuamo'o and Hawai'i (December 20).

1820—Liholiho, at the behest of Ka'ahumanu, orders the burning of all ki'i (symbolic images) in temples and shrines.

Chronology of Important Events

- —First company of American missionaries to Hawai'i (out of Boston, on the brig *Thaddeus*) sight the Island of Hawai'i, March 30, depositing a portion of the missionary group at Kailua, April 4, before continuing to Honolulu, where the *Thaddeus* drops anchor April 14, leaving Honolulu's first group of Congregationalist missionaries.
- —The *Maro*, (out of Nantucket, Joseph Allen, master) first whaleship to enter Honolulu harbor arrives.

1821—First Christian service held in Honolulu, April 24; first (thatched) church dedicated, September 15, on site makai of present Kawaiaha'o Church.

1822—Work begins on development of a written Hawaiian language; first printing done in the Hawaiian Islands on mission press, January 7.

1823—Liholiho, Queen Kamāmalu, and attendants, sail for England in English whaler *L'Aigle*, leaving Ka'ahumanu as regent in charge of the kingdom (November 27).
- —Ka'ahumanu establishes civil code—influenced by missionary teachings—prohibiting murder, theft, fighting, and Sabbath-breaking.

1824—Queen Kamāmalu dies in London, July 8, followed by King Kamehameha II, July 14.
- —High Chiefess Kapi'olani, as an act of Christian faith, descends into Kīlauea crater, where in defiance of the volcano goddess Pele, she shouts "Jehovah is my God." (December) Thereafter, Christian converts increase.

1825—In early may, High Chief Boki returns from England on the British Royal Navy frigate *Blonde*, Capt. George Anson Byron master, with the bodies of Kamehameha II and his wife Kamāmalu, both of whom had died of measles in London.
- —Kauikeaouli is proclaimed ruler as Kamehameha III, under the regency of Ka'ahumanu (June 6).

1828—On December 29, under Boki's leadership, the brig *Kamehameha*, together with Beckett (both of Hawaiian registry), leave Honolulu on expedition to the south in search of sandalwood. Beckett returns August 3, 1830, with news that *Kamehameha* and all on board were mysteriously lost.

1832—Ka'ahumamu, favorite wife of Kamehameha I and kuhina nui for Kamehameha II and Kamehameha III, dies on May 5, in Mānoa Valley. Born circa 1773, she was about 59. High Chiefess Kīna'u is appointed kuhina nui in June.

1833—Kamehameha III, at nineteen, assumes reins of government, but the following year turns over many governing powers to Kīna'u, confirming her in the post of kuhina nui (March).

1835—Ladd & Co. begins sugar planting at Kōloa, Kaua'i.
- —Princess Nahi'ena'ena, sister of Kamehameha II and Kamehameha III, marries Leleiōhoku I and dies the following year at Lahaina, Maui.

1837—Kamehameha III marries Hakaleleponi Kalama Kapakuhaili, on or about February 2.
- —Laying out of the public streets of Honolulu begins.

1839—Kamehameha III proclaims the Declaration of Rights (June 7).
- —French frigate *L'Artemise*, Post Captain Laplace in command, arrives July 9, and before leaving July 20 forces Hawaiian government to sign treaty guaranteeing complete religious freedom for Catholics.

1840—At the request, in May 1839, of Kamehameha III and chiefs, to the Protestant mission that a family educate young chiefs, Amos Starr and Juliette Montague Cooke establish the Hawaiian Chief's School, with dedication ceremonies April 15.
- —Kamehameha III establishes Hawai'i's first written constitution.

1842—The Rev. William Richards, with High Chief Ha'alilio, private secretary and business manager for Kamehameha III, go on diplomatic mission, seeking equitable treaties and recognition of independence from the United States, France, and Great Britain, sailing on the schooner *Shaw* (July 8).
- —By the end of the year, the United States, under President John Tyler, recognizes independence of Hawaiian kingdom. (December 19.)

1843—England's Lord George Paulet, seizes Hawaiian Islands; Kamehameha III cedes kingdom (February 25), the English flag is raised.

—Admiral Richard Thomas of the British navy repudiates Paulet's action, restoring sovereignty to Hawai'i, following Queen Victoria's intervention on behalf of Hawai'i (July).

—On Restoration Day, July 31, at Thanksgiving service at Kawaiaha'o Church, Kamehameha III speaks briefly, making the statement that becomes the national motto of Hawai'i: "Ua mau ke ea o ka āina i ka pono" ("The life of the land is preserved in righteousness").

—Great Britain and France sign dual agreement recognizing "the Sandwich Islands an independent state," (November 28).

1844—Construction begins on palace that would serve five Hawaiian monarchs and eventually be known as "Old 'Iolani Palace," when torn down, 1878, to make way for the new 'Iolani Palace begun 1879.

1845—Representatives first chosen from the commoners under constitution of October 1840 (April 2).

—First legislature is convened by Kamehameha III (May 20).

1846—New treaties are concluded with Great Britain and France (March 26).

—Washington Place, a Greek Revival house for American sea captain John Dominis, is built, later becoming the home of future Queen Lili'uokalani, when she marries Dominis' son, John Owen Dominis.

1848—Kamehameha III enacts the "Mahele" (also called "The Great Mahele"), a division of lands, creating fee-simple land ownership. Over next three years, land is divided among ali'i, the government, and native tenants, with foreigners granted the right to own land.

—Attempts at Reciprocity with the United States are made by J. J. Jarves (October 26 and November 23).

1848-1849—Epidemics kill thousands—one-tenth of Hawaiian population.

1849—Honolulu fort is seized by Admiral Tromelin, of the French navy, and partially destroyed (August 25).

—Princes Royal, Alexander Liholiho and Lot Kapuāiwa, embark for the United States accompanied by Dr. G. P. Judd (September 11).

1850—Honolulu is declared a city, and the capital of the kingdom. Treaty between United States and Hawai'i is ratified.

—High Chiefess Bernice Pauahi marries Charles Reed Bishop, June 4, although betrothed to Lot Kamehameha.

1851—Protectorate is offered to the United States (March 10).

—First whale oil and bone are transshipped. Treaty with Great Britain (July 10)

1852—Kamehameha III grants second Constitution of Hawai'i (June 14).

1853—Smallpox (ma'i pu'upu'u li'ili'i) sweeps over Hawai'i in waves from February into January 1854, with 5,405 cases reported, including 2,485 deaths.

—First Hawaiian postage stamps are issued.

1854—Kamehameha III dies (December 15).

—Alexander Liholiho, inaugurated January 11, 1855 as Kamehameha IV.

1855—Victoria Kamāmalu, younger sister of Kamehameha IV and Kamehameha V, at sixteen, is named kuhina nui on or about January 16; as the last kuhina nui she serves until August 13, 1864.

—Second effort for Reciprocity Treaty with United States. A treaty is signed but not ratified (July 20).

1856—Kamehameha IV and Emma Rooke marry at Kawaiaha'o Church (June 19).

1857—Honolulu Fort is demolished.

1858—The birth of Albert Edward Kauikeaouli, Prince of Hawai'i (Ka Haku o Hawai'i), son of Kamehameha IV and Queen Emma, in Honolulu (May 20).

—New treaty with France concluded (September 8).

1860—The Queen's Hospital (named in honor of Queen Emma, who took a personal interest in funding the project) is completed (December).

1862—Death of Albert Edward Kauikeaouli, Prince of Hawai'i (August 27).

1863—Death of Kamehameha IV, November 30, at twenty-nine.
- —Prince Lot Kamehameha ascends the throne as Kamehameha V (November 30).
- —David Kalākaua marries Kapiʻolani II (December 19).

1864—The third Constitution of Hawaiʻi takes effect.

1865—Royal Order of Kamehameha I is founded (April 11).
- —Removal of remains of kings and queens buried on ʻIolani Palace grounds tomb to Mauna ʻAla (Nuʻuanu Mausoleum) (October 30).
- —Death of Victoria Kamāmalu (May 29).

1867—Effort toward a Reciprocity Treaty with the United States is renewed.

1871—In the fall, the loss of thirty-three ships of the Arctic whaling fleet—added to other problems associated with the industry—proves to be a fatal blow to commercial whaling.

1872—On his death bed, Kamehameha V offers the throne to Bernice Pauahi; she refuses the crown, and Lot dies at forty-two without an heir (December 11).
- —At the request of Kamehameha V, Kaiser Wilhelm sends Captain Henri Berger, a Prussian army officer, to direct "His Majesty's Hawaiian band"; Berger arrives June 2 and establishes what becomes the Royal Hawaiian Band, still in existence in 2005.

1873—Prince William Charles Lunalilo is elected king by the legislature at a special session (January 8).
- —Renewed effort for Reciprocity Treaty with the United States, this time offering the cession of Pearl Harbor as a naval base. Offer is later withdrawn.
- —Abolition of the army, by royal command (September 12).

1874—King Lunalilo dies at thirty-nine, in Honolulu, without issue and without naming an heir (January 8).
- —Prince David Kalākaua at a special session of the legislature, is elected king (February 12).
- —Riot at the Court House by anti-Kalākaua forces favoring election of Queen Emma is quelled by armed forces from American and British warships (February 12).
- —King Kalākaua takes oath of office at Kīnaʻu Hale (February 13).
- —Kalākaua names his younger brother William Pitt Leleʻiōhoku II successor to the throne (February 14).
- —Efforts to establish a Reciprocity Treaty with the United States (October 18).
- —King Kalākaua with others travels to the United States in support of Reciprocity efforts in November
- —Aliʻiolani Hale opens.

1875—Return of King Kalākaua on the USS *Pensacola* (February 15).
- —Remains of King Lunalilo are placed in mausoleum at Kawaiahaʻo church.

1876—Reciprocity Treaty between United States and Hawaiian Kingdom is ratified due in part to Kalākaua's recent visit; Hawaiian raw sugar may now enter the United States free of duty (August 13).

1878—Liliʻuokalani composes *Aloha ʻOe*.

1879—Cornerstone of ʻIolani Palace is laid under Masonic auspices (December 31).

1881—King Kalākaua sets out on world tour, becoming first head of state in history to circumnavigate the globe.
- —Cornerstone laid for Lunalilo Home, for aged and indigent Hawaiians, established according to the will of King Lunalilo.
- —King Kalākaua returns from trip around the world.

1882—ʻIolani Palace is completed.

1883—Statue of Kamehameha the Great unveiled in Honolulu (February).
- —Coronation of King Kalākaua and Queen Kapiʻolani; revival of hula at coronation (February 12).
- —Death of Princess Ruth Keʻelikolani, granddaughter of Kamehameha I and heir to royal lands following death of Kamehameha V (May 24).
- —United States Congress refuses to renew the Reciprocity Treaty.

1884—Death of Bernice Pauahi Bishop, great-granddaughter of Kamehameha I (October 16); her fortune endows the Kamehameha Schools for Boys and Girls.

1885—The *City of Tokyo* bringing Japanese immigrant laborers arrives at Honolulu (February 8), and they are entertained by hula dancers and King Kalākaua welcomes them personally.

—Queen Emma, granddaughter of John Young, blood relative to Kamehameha I, widow of Kamehameha IV, dies (April 25).

1886—Jubilee celebration of King Kalākaua's fiftieth birthday (November 16).

—Kalākaua sends John Bush to Samoa to attempt to build a Polynesian Confederacy. The proposal initially meets with success but threats by Germany extinguish it.

1887—Queen Kapiʻolani and Princess Liliʻuokalani visit England to attend Queen Victoria's Diamond Jubilee.

—Great political mass meeting held in Honolulu to request a new constitution and to demand the dismissal of Walter M. Gibson's ministry (June 30).

—Kalākaua is forced to sign the "Bayonet Constitution," which limits his power and the voting rights of the Hawaiian people (July 7).

—Hawaiʻi extends the Treaty of Reciprocity with the United States for several years by allowing American warships the right to enter Pearl Harbor as a coaling and repair base.

1889—Princess Kaʻiulani departs for England to finish her education (May 10).

—Insurrection of R. W. Wilcox and his party of malcontents are quickly subdued; six insurgents are killed, twelve are wounded, and the rest surrender (July 30).

1890—King Kalākaua departs Honolulu on the USS *Charleston* for San Francisco, to improve his health. Princess Liliʻuokalani is appointed regent of the kingdom (November 25).

1891—King Kalākaua dies in San Francisco, aged fifty-four (January 20).

—Kalākaua's remains arrive at Honolulu on the *Charleston*. Liliʻuokalani becomes Queen of the Hawaiian Islands (January 29).

—State funeral of King Kalākaua (February 15).

—Cabinet resigns at request of the queen, who appoints a new ministry (February 25).

—Princess Kaʻiulani, niece of the queen, is proclaimed heir apparent (March 9).

—John Dominis, Prince Consort, dies at Washington Place, Honolulu, at age sixty (August 27).

1893—Queen Liliʻuokalani attempts to abrogate the constitution and proclaim a new one, but is thwarted by her ministers. Citizens organize Committee of Safety (January 14).

—Mass meeting at the Armory confirms the Committee of Safety organization and empowers it "to devise such ways and means as may be necessary to secure the permanent maintenance of law and order and the protection of life, liberty and property in Hawaii." Marines from the USS *Boston* are landed at 5 p.m. (January 16).

—Committee of Safety takes possession of the government building, deposing Liliʻuokalani and proclaims the monarchial system of government abrogated; a provisional government is established, Sanford B. Dole president (January 17).

—Special commission leaves for Washington to negotiate a Treaty of Annexation (January 19).

—United States Minister Stevens, at the request of the Provisional Government, proclaims a United States protectorate over Hawaiʻi, pending results at Washington. An American flag is hoisted over the government building (February 1).

—Annexation treaty is signed at Washington; submitted to the Senate by U.S. President Benjamin Harrison (February 14).

—Grover Cleveland becomes U.S. president (March 4).

—Arrival in Honolulu of Colonel James H. Blount to investigate the overthrow (March 27).

—Commissioner Blount orders the lowering of the American flag and the return of all naval forces to their warships.

Chronology of Important Events

- —U.S. Minister Willis arrives in Honolulu to open negotiations with Liliʻuokalani with a view to her restoration (November 4).
- —Mass meeting in Honolulu to protest President Cleveland's plan to restore Liliʻuokalani (November 25).
- —U.S. Minister Willis informs President Dole that the United States is prepared to arbitrate on the behalf of Liliʻuokalani and notes that she was deposed through the aid of United States forces; he requests that the Provisional Government restore the Queen's authority (December 19).
- —President Dole declines to accede; refuses U.S. President Cleveland's right of self-assumed arbitrament (December 23).

1894—Republic of Hawaii is established, ending royal rule (July 4). Sanford B. Dole president.

1895—Group of Hawaiians under leadership of Sam Nowlein and R. W. Wilcox, arming to overthrow the government and restore Liliʻuokalani, is surprised at dusk at Diamond Head (January 6).
- —Battle of Mānoa Valley; three royalists are killed, other rebels escape (January 9).
- —Sam Nowlein and three aides are captured. Wilcox found in Kalihi fishing hut (January 14).
- —Liliʻuokalani arrested and confined to the executive building, formerly ʻIolani Palace (January 16).
- —Liliʻuokalani sends to President Dole her abdication and renunciation of all sovereign rights, admits and declares the Republic of Hawaiʻi to be the lawful government to which she certifies her oath of allegiance (January 24).
- —Liliʻuokalani, appearing before the Military Commission for trial, is charged with misprision of treason (February 15); she is found "guilty as charged"; sentenced to imprisonment at hard labor for five years and fined $5,000 (February 27)—said sentence never executed.
- —Liliʻuokalani is paroled, subject to restriction of movement, and returns to Washington Place (September 6).

1896—Restriction on movements of Liliʻuokalani are removed (February 7).

1897—Princess Kaʻiulani returns from abroad after absence of over eight years (November 9).

1898—Hawaiʻi is annexed, August 12—sometimes called "Flag raising" day—when President Dole formally cedes jurisdiction and property of the Hawaiian Government to the United States; the Hawaiian government, under the American flag, is to continue as a republic until a commission decides on the form of government for Hawaiʻi. The interim government continues with Dole governing as president.

1899—Death of Princess Victoria Kaʻiulani, at twenty-four (March 6).
- —Death of Queen Kapiʻolani, widow of King Kalākaua (June 24).

1900—Hawaiʻi territorial government established; Sanford B. Dole appointed governor by U.S. President William McKinley (June 14).
- —R. W. Wilcox is elected first delegate to Congress from Hawaiʻi.

1902—Prince Jonah Kūhiō Kalanianaʻole, titular prince of the former monarchy, is elected delegate to U.S. Congress, as Republican.

1903—Robert Wilcox, revolutionist, dies.

1909—New royal mausoleum crypt for bodies of members of the Kalākaua dynasty is completed.

1917—Liliʻuokalani, former Queen of Hawaiʻi, dies at Washington Place (November 11).
- —State funeral of Liliʻuokalani (November 18).

1919—Kamehameha Day, one hundredth anniversary of death of Kamehameha the Great, is observed with historical procession (June 11).

1921—Hawaiian Homes Act is passed by Congress, providing for Hawaiian Homes Commission, to set apart territorial lands for Hawaiians.
- —Historic ʻĀinahau, home of Princess Likelike and her daughter, Princess Kaʻiulani, burns (August 2).

1922—Prince Jonah Kalanianaʻole, last titular prince of the monarchy, nephew of King Kalākaua, delegate to Congress from Hawaiʻi for twenty years, dies in Waikīkī (January 7).

1993—ʻOnipaʻa, commemoration of the 1893 overthrow of the monarchy, is observed.

2004—Akaka Bill sponsored by U.S. Representative Daniel Akaka seeks recognition of sovereign rights of Hawaiʻi's indigenous people.

BIBLIOGRAPHY

Allen, Helena, *The Betrayal of Liliuokalani*, Arthur H. Clark, Glendale: 1982.

Armstrong, William, *Around the World with a King*, Stokes Company, New York: 1904.

Bailey, Paul, *Those Kings and Queens of Old Hawaii*, Westernlore Press, Tuscon: 1988.

Beckwith, Martha, *Hawaiian Mythology*, University of Hawai'i Press, Honolulu: 1982

Beckwith, Martha, translator, *The Kumulipo*, University of Hawai'i Press, Honolulu: 1990.

Berger, Andrew, *Hawaiian Birdlife*, University of Hawai'i Press, Honolulu: 1981.

Buck, Peter, *Vikings of the Pacific*, University of Chicago Press, Chicago: 1972.

Burns, Eugene, *The Last King of Paradise*, Pellegrini & Cudahy, New York: 1952.

Bushnell, O. A., *Ka'a'awa*, University of Hawai'i Press, Honolulu: 1972.

Cordy, Ross, *Exalted Sits the Chief*, Mutual Publishing, Honolulu: 2000.

—— *An Ancient History of Wai'anae*, Mutual Publishing, Honolulu: 2002.

Daws, Gavan, *Shoal of Time*, University of Hawai'i Press, Honolulu: 1982.

Day, A. Grove, *History Makers of Hawaii*, Mutual Publishing, Honolulu: 1984.

Elbert, Samuel H., ed., *Selections from Fornander's Hawaiian Antiquities and Folklore*, University of Hawai'i Press, Honolulu: 1982.

Ellis, William, *Narrative of a Tour Through Hawaii in 1823*, Charles E. Tuttle, Rutland: 1979.

Emory, Kenneth, *Religion in Ancient Hawaii, Aspects of Hawaiian Life and Environment*, The Kamehameha Schools Press, Honolulu: 1965.

Feher, Joseph, *Hawaii: A Pictorial History*, Bishop Museum Press, Honolulu: 1969.

Forbes, David, *Encounters with Paradise*, Honolulu Academy of Arts, Honolulu: 1992.

Goldman, Irving, *Ancient Polynesian Society*, University of Chicago Press, Chicago: 1970.

Grant, Glen and Bennett Hymer, *Hawai'i Looking Back*, Mutual Publishing, Honolulu: 2000.

Holt, John Dominis, *Monarchy in Hawaii*, Topgallant Publishing, Honolulu: 1971.

Ii, John Papa, *Fragments of Hawaiian History*, Bishop Museum Press, Honolulu: 1959.

Joesting, Edward, *Kauai: The Separate Kingdom*, University of Hawai'i Press, Honolulu: 1987.

Kaeppler, Adrienne, ed., *Cook Voyage Artifacts*, Bishop Museum Press, Honolulu: 1978.

Kalākaua, David, *The Legends and Myths of Hawaii*, Charles E. Tuttle, Rutland: 1974.

Kamae, Lori, *The Empty Throne*, Topgallant Publishing, Honolulu: 1980.

Kamakau, Samuel, *Ruling Chiefs of Hawaii*, Kamehameha Schools Press, Honolulu: 1992.

—— *The Works of the People of Old*, Bishop Museum Press, Honolulu: 1976.

Kanahele, George, *Ku Kanaka Stand Tall*, University of Hawaiʻi Press, Honolulu: 1986.

Kanahele, George, ed., *Hawaiian Music and Musicians*, University of Hawaiʻi Press, Honolulu: 1979.

Kane, Herb Kawainui, *Voyage: The Discovery of Hawaii*, Island Heritage, Honolulu: 1976.

Kane, Herb Kawainui, *Voyagers*, WhaleSong, Bellevue: 1991.

Korn, Alfons, ed., *News From Molokai: Letters Between Peter Kaeo and Queen Emma*, University of Hawaiʻi Press, Honolulu: 1976.

Kuykendall, Ralph, *The Hawaiian Kingdom*, vol. 1, University of Hawaiʻi Press, Honolulu: 1965.

—— *The Hawaiian Kingdom*, vol. 2, University of Hawaiʻi Press, Honolulu: 1966.

Kuykendall, Ralph, *The Hawaiian Kingdom*, vol. 3, University of Hawaii Press, Honolulu: 1967.

Liliʻuokalani, *Hawaii's Story By Hawaii's Queen*, Charles E. Tuttle, Rutland: 1898.

Malo, David, *Hawaiian Antiquities*, Bishop Museum Press, Honolulu: 1991.

McKinzie, Edith Kawalohea, *Hawaiian Genealogies*, vol. 1, Institute for Polynesian Studies, Lāʻie: 1983.

—— *Hawaiian Genealogies*, vol. 2, Institute for Polynesian Studies, Lāʻie: 1986.

Mitchell, Donald, ed., *Resource Units in Hawaiian Culture*, Kamehameha Schools Press, Honolulu: 1986.

Murray-Oliver, Anthony, *Captain Cook's Hawaii as Seen by His Artists*, Millwood Press, Wellington: 1975.

Nakanaela, Thomas, *Biography of Robert Kalanihiapo Wilcox*, unpublished English translation by Martha Webb: 1986.

Pukui, Mary Kawena, *Olelo Noʻeau*, Bishop Museum Press, Honolulu: 1983.

Pukui, Mary Kawena and Samuel Elbert, *Hawaiian Dictionary*, University of Hawaiʻi Press, Honolulu: 1977.

Pukui, Mary Kawena, Samuel Elbert, and Esther Mookini, *Place Names of Hawaii*, University of Hawaiʻi Press, Honolulu: 1976.

Rose, Roger, *Hawaiʻi: The Royal Isles*, Bishop Museum Press, Honolulu: 1980.

Russ, William, *The Hawaiian Revolution*, Susquehanna University Press, Selinsgrove: 1959.

—— *The Hawaiian Republic*, Susquehanna University Press, Selinsgrove: 1961.

Sinclair, Marjorie, *Nahienaena*, University of Hawaiʻi Press, Honolulu: 1976.

Sobrero, Gina, *An Italian Baroness in Hawaiʻi*, Hawaiian Historical Society, Honolulu: 1991.

Spoehr, Anne Harding, *The Royal Lineages of Hawaiʻi*, Bishop Museum Press, Honolulu: 1989.

Swenson, J., *Treasures of the Hawaiian Kingdom*, Tongg Publishing, Honolulu: 1979.

Stannard, David, *Before the Horror*, Social Science Research Institute, University of Hawaiʻi, Honolulu: 1989.

Tregaskis, Richard, *The Warrior King*, Macmillan Publishing, New York: 1973.

Westervelt, W. D., *Myths and Legends of Hawaiʻi*, Mutual Publishing, Honolulu: 1987.

Wisniewski, Richard, *The Rise and Fall of the Hawaiian Kingdom*, Pacific Basin Enterprises, Honolulu: 1979.

Zambucka, Kristin, *Kalakaua: Hawaiʻi's Last King*, Mana Publishing, Honolulu: 1983.

PHOTO CREDITS

ALLAN SEIDEN
ix: right; 2: top; 4: top; 7: center right, bottom right; 8: bottom left, right; 9: top; 32; 39: bottom; 77: top; 101; 105: top; 112: all; 113; 118: all; 121

ALLAN SEIDEN from the collections of the BISHOP MUSEUM
9: bottom; 11: top; 14: bottom

ALLAN SEIDEN from the collections of the HAWAI'I STATE ARCHIVES
x: right; xi: left, center; 19: top, bottom; 23; 25: all; 27: all; 28; 30: bottom; 35; 36: bottom; 37; 38; 40; 42: top left, bottom; 46; 48: left; 49; 50: all; 52; 53; 54: all; 55: all; 57; 58: top; 66; 73; 76; 78: bottom; 79: bottom; 84; 98-99; 100; 102: top and bottom; 103, all; 105: bottom; 109; 115: all; 116; 117: top, center

ALLAN SEIDEN from the DON MEDCALF COLLECTION
11: bottom; 26: bottom; 58: bottom; 72; 95: left; 117: bottom

ALLAN SEIDEN from PRIVATE COLLECTIONS
vii: right; ix: left; 2: bottom; 3: bottom left; 5: all; 8: center left; 14: top; 39: top; 47; 65: bottom; 75: bottom

ALLAN SEIDEN from the ROYAL LEGACY ARCHIVES
ix: center

BAKER-VAN DYKE COLLECTION
60: all; 61: all; 62; 92, all

BISHOP MUSEUM
iv-v; iv-v; xi, Hedemann Collection; 7: top right; 10: top, bottom; 12; 14: center right and left; 18; 20: bottom; 22; 24: top; 29; 31: top; 33: all; 34; 41; 42: top right; 43; 56. Dickson Collection; 63; 65: top, center; 77: center; 79: top; 80: all; 81: top; 83: bottom right, Gonsalves Collection; 85, Dickson Collection; 87: center and bottom left, Chase Collection; 90-91, Gonsalves Collection; 94, Davey Collection; 97: top, Davey Collection; 102: center; 106: center, Hedemann Collection; 106: bottom

DIXSON LIBRARY (STATE LIBRARY OF NEW SOUTH WALES, AUSTRALIA)
vii: left; 3: top right

HAWAIIAN HISTORICAL SOCIETY
x: left; 1: center; 26: top; 31: bottom

HAWAIIAN HISTORICAL SOCIETY
71: top, bottom left; 81: bottom, Annie M. Parke Collection; 95: right; 96

HAWAI'I STATE ARCHIVES
1: right; 21; 59: left, top right; 59: bottom right, Chase Collection; 64; 67: all; 69; 70; 71: bottom right; 77: bottom; 78: top; 82: all; 83: top, bottom left; 87: top left, right, bottom right; 89, all; 93; 97: bottom; 98-99, 107; 114

HONOLULU ACADEMY OF ARTS
13; 17: top; 24: bottom; 36: top; 48: right; 75: top

RAE HUO
30: top, from the collections of the Bishop Museum

HERB KANE
vii: center, collection of Charles and Mavis Lavin; x: center, collection of Cathy Bechtel Reed; 1: left, collection of King Kamehameha's Kona Resort Hotel; 3: bottom right, collection of Jewel Rose; 4: bottom, collection of Jay Rose; 15: top, collection of Cathy Bechtel Reed; 15: bottom, collection of Mr. and Mrs. Richard Cox; 16: top, collection of

National Park Service; 16: bottom, collection of Nick G. Maggos; 17: bottom, collection of King Kamehameha's Kona Resort Hotel; 44, collection of Charles and Mavis Lavin; 45, collection of artist

ELIZABETH PA MARTIN
119: all

PEABODY MUSEUM OF SALEM
20: top; 74

DOUGLAS PEEBLES
108; 120: all

DOUGLAS RISEBOROUGH
6, collection of Grand Hyatt Wailea

QUEEN'S MEDICAL CENTER
110; 111

SCIENTIFIC RESEARCH MUSEUM (ST. PETERSBURG, RUSSIA)
7: bottom left; 8: top left

INDEX

A

Adams, USS, 58
Aea, Kaipo, 97
ʻAhahui Kaʻahumanu, 120
Aholo, Lydia K., 96, 97
ʻahuʻula, ix, 6, 7
ʻaikapu, ix
ʻAimoku, Limiki, 97
ʻāina, ix, 43, 85
ʻĀinahau, 101, 105, 106, 107
Akaka Bill, 128
Akaka, Daniel, 128
aliʻi, viii, ix, x, xi, xii, xiii, 2, 3, 4, 5, 6, 7, 8, 9, 11, 13, 15, 17, 19, 20, 21, 23, 24, 25, 26, 27, 29, 37, 43, 45, 46, 47, 48, 49, 50, 51, 52, 54, 55, 57, 62, 68, 70, 74, 75, 77, 85, 86, 97, 101, 103, 109, 110, 111, 114, 116, 117, 121, 124
aliʻi nui, viii, ix, xi, xii, xiii, 4, 10, 13, 14, 16, 85
Aliʻiolani Hale, vi
Aloha ʻOe, 85, 93
American Civil War, 37
ancient Hawaiʻi, xii, 2, 4
annexation, 27, 30, 54, 66, 80, 88, 92, 93, 104, 107, 114, 115, 127
Annexationist Club, 86, 88
Armstrong, William N., 62, 63
around the world trip, 62, 126
Around the World with a King, 63

B

Babbit, Sarah, 95
Battle of Nuʻuanu Valley, 9, 14
Bayonet Constitution, 68, 70, 85, 86, 92, 127
Becket, 47
Beechey, Richard, 74
Bensell, C. E., 20
Bertelman, Henry, 59
bird catchers, 7
birds 6, 7, 8

Bishop, Bernice Pauahi, vi, xiii, 41, 55, 68, 82, 126
  Charles Reed, 35, 55, 80, 81, 125
  Estate, 111
  Museum, 7, 8, 9, 14, 30, 55
  Sereno E., 88
Blonde, HMS, 21, 124
Blount, James H., xi, 88, 93, 104
Board of Immigration, 37
Boki, 7, 21, 47, 48, 124
Boston, USS, 88, 127
Boyd, Edwin, 93
  John, 59, 116
British, 2, 10, 21, 24, 25, 27, 29, 31, 51, 52, 55, 57, 68, 77, 86, 101, 117, 122, 124, 125
  Foreign Office, 27
  Royal Navy, 122, 124
Bush, John, 71, 127

C

Campbell, Abigail Wahiikaʻahuʻula, 116
  Estate, 116
  James, 116
Carter, J. O., 95
Charleston, USS, 63, 126
Chiefs' Children's School, 24, 29, 31, 51, 55, 57, 85, 86
chief's house, 75
Chinese, 27, 30, 37, 58
Choris, Louis, 13, 14, 17, 45, 46, 75
Cleghorn, Annie, 101, 105
  Archibald, 55, 101, 103, 104
Cleveland, Grover, xi, 54, 88, 104, 127
Committee of Safety, 88, 102, 127
commoners, x, 3, 5, 6, 23, 27, 37
Congress, United States, xiii, 88, 93, 104, 114, 116, 127, 128
consort, vi, 31, 52, 67, 89, 127
constitution, 25, 66, 68, 86, 88, 92, 124, 125, 126, 127

Constitution of 1840, 25
   of 1852, 25
   of 1864, 126
Cook, Capt. James, 2, 3, 4, 6, 14, 27, 122
   Monument, 60
coronation, 10, 11, 53, 59, 66, 67, 114, 126
   Ball, 66
Crown Lands , 19, 26, 53
Cummins, John A., 50, 91

D

Daughters of Hawai'i, 76, 77
Davis, Isaac, 14, 15
   Isaac Young, 55
disease , 5, 8, 21, 23, 26, 27, 30, 37, 109
dissent, 62
Dole, Sanford, xi, 94, 96, 127, 128
Dominis, John 'Aimoku, 81, 126
   John Owen, 81, 85, 89
   Lydia Kamaka'eha, 82, 87
   Mary, 81

E

education, 20, 24, 29, 31, 51, 86, 104, 109, 111, 112, 127
Edward, Prince of Wales ,117
election, xiii, 10, 41, 52, 57, 58, 60, 68, 86
England, xii, 21, 48, 52, 53, 54, 55, 70, 102, 103, 106, 114, 116, 123, 125

F

Fair American, 14, 15
feather ix, x, xiii, 3, 6, 7, 8, 9, 10, 11, 14, 69, 120, 122
   cloak, ix, 6, 9, 10, 66
   work, 6
Fornander, Abraham, 14
fort, 20, 123, 125
Fort Street 36
France, 27, 30, 53, 66, 124, 125

G

Gardinier, Gertrude, 101, 102
Gibson, Walter Murray, xi, 66, 70, 127
Golovnin, Vasili, 13
Great Britain, 21, 27, 30, 66, 122, 124, 125
Great Harrowden Hall, 102, 104
Great Māhele, x, 26, 78, 85, 125

H

hale, ix, 20, 51, 75, 78
Hale o Keawe, 2
hānai, ix, 29, 51, 52, 80, 85, 96, 97
Hānaiakamalama, 77
Hawai'i Pono'i, 64, 102
Hawai'i's Story by Hawai'i's Queen, 94
Hawaiian coat of arms, 10
   flag, 96, 123
   Homes Act, 128
   Homes Commission, 114, 128
   independence, xi, 27, 51, 54, 62, 70, 80, 86, 109, 116
   Islands, viii, 21, 67, 92, 107, 122, 125
   Kingdom, 1, 5, 13, 14, 15, 16, 17, 19, 23. 25, 26, 27, 29, 30, 31, 46, 49, 50, 52, 53, 55, 62, 66, 68, 69, 70, 71, 81, 85, 86, 96, 107, 110
   language, ix, 24, 68, 124
   League, The, 66
heiau, ix, xii, 14, 16, 20, 21, 82, 121, 123
Helumoa, 82, 83
Hillebrand, William, 30
Holt, John D., 59
Honolulu Fort, 31, 80, 125
   Harbor, vi, 52, 58, 82, 122, 123
hospital, 26, 30, 52, 54, 109, 110
House of Nobles, 5, 25, 57, 80
hula, x, 2, 6, 11, 57, 64, 65, 67, 79, 82
Hulihe'e Palace, 51, 76, 78
Hymn of Kamehameha I, 62

I

I'i, John, 80
immigrants, 127
International Marketplace, 83
'Iolani Palace, vi, 10, 11, 51, 66, 67, 69, 70, 75, 78, 88, 93, 101, 107, 117, 119

J

Japan, 62, 63, 66, 68, 104
Japanese, 27, 104, 106, 127
Joy Cloak, 7
Judd 25, 26, 29
   Charles H., 62, 63
   Dr. Gerrit P., xi, vii, 25, 30, 52, 125

K

Ka 'Imiloa, 71
ka mō'ī, ix, 10
Ka'ahumanu, xi, 17, 19, 20, 21, 23, 45, 46, 47, 48, 49, 50, 75, 76

Index | 134

kāʻai kapu o Līloa, x, 8
Kahekili, xi, 13, 14, 16, 123
kāhili, ix, 9, 10, 11, 50, 66, 69, 96, 97
kāhuna, ix, 2, 14, 46, 86
Kailua-Kona, 13, 14, 17, 60, 76, 78
Kaʻiulani, Victoria, vi, vii, xi, xiii, 55, 62, 83, 91, 95, 101, 102, 103, 104,, 105, 106, 107
Kalākaua, David, vi, xi, xii, xiii, 10, 11, 27, 32, 41, 51, 54, 55, 58, 62, 68, 75, 78, 82, 83, 109, 110, 114, 117, 126, 127, 128
Kalama, Queen, xii, 27, 31, 47, 48, 124
Kalanianaʻole, Jonah Kūhiō, vi, xi, 114, 115
Kalanimōkū, 20, 21, 23, 50, 123
Kalaninui, Keōua Kupuapā, 13
Kalaniʻōpuʻu, xi, xii, xiii, 4, 13, 14
Kalola, 47
Kamakaʻeha, Lydia, vii, 85, 86, 87, 98
Kamakau, Samuel, xii, 24
Kamāmalu, Queen Victoria, x, xiii, 21, 32, 38, 124, 125, 126
Kamehameha
    the Great, vi, viii, x, xi, xii, xiii, 3, 6, 8, 9, 11, 13, 14, 15, 16, 17, 19, 29, 50, 6, 8, 11, 14, 19, 29, 46, 47, 50, 51, 54, 55, 66, 76, 80, 82, 86, 101, 122, 123, 125, 126, 128
    the Second, vi, x, xi, xii, xiii, 9, 11, 19, 20, 21, 23, 46, 47, 48, 52, 54, 75, 123, 124
    the Third, vi, viii, ix, x, xi, xii, xiii, 5, 10, 23, 24, 25, 26, 27, 29, 31, 46, 47, 48, 49, 50, 52, 75, 77, 80, 81, 85, 103, 124, 125
    the Fourth, vi, x, xii, xiii, 28, 29, 30, 31, 33, 35, 51, 52, 57, 62, 75, 76, 77, 110, 125, 126
    the Fifth (Lot), vi, x, xii, xiii, 11, 31, 34, 35, 36, 37, 39, 41, 42, 49, 52, 53, 54, 55, 57, 64, 75, 77, 79, 82, 83, 103, 126
    Day, 128
    Day Parade ,112
    Schools, xiii, 55, 111, 112, 127
    School for Boys, 111
    statue of, 67
Kanaʻina, Charles, 43, 109
Kāne, Hoapili, 47
Kapiʻolani, vi, xi, xii, 10, 32, 53, 54, 59, 62, 66, 67, 69, 109, 114, 117
    Abigail, 116
    Maternity Hospital and the Home for Leper Girls, 54
Kapoukahi, 14
kapu, viii, ix, x, 5, 9, 10, 11, 19, 20, 21, 25, 45, 46, 47, 54, 122, 123
kauhale, x
Kauikeaouli, Albert Edward, vii, xii, 19, 20, 23, 24, 27, 30, 46, 47, 52, 124
Kaumualiʻi, xii, 9, 46, 53, 123

Kawaiahaʻo Church, 20, 29, 41, 43, 49, 82, 98, 124, 125
Kawānanakoa, Abigail Campbell, 117
    Abigail Kinoiki Kekaulike, 117
    Andrew Piʻikoi, 117
    David, vi, xii, 104, 105, 114, 116
    Edward, 114, 116, 117
    Elizabeth, 117
    Regina Keōpūolani, 117
Kealakekua Bay, 3, 4, 6, 21, 60, 122
Keʻeaumoku, 45, 122
Keʻelikōlani, Princess Ruth, xii, 50, 51, 52, 55, 68, 76, 78, 83, 101
Kekaulike, Abigail Kinoiki, 114, 117
Kekāuluohi, Miriam, 42
Kekūanaōʻa, Mataio, xii, xiii, 26, 29, 32, 38, 50
Kekuiapoiwa, 13
Keōuahale, 51, 78
Keōpūolani, xii, xiii, 17, 19, 45, 46, 47, 48, 117, 123
Keōua, xii, 45, 101, 122
Kīnaʻu, xii, xiii, 5, 23, 25, 27, 29, 45, 48, 49, 50, 51, 85
    John Pitt, 50
    William Pitt, 51
Kīwalaʻō, xii, xiii, 47
Kuakini, John Adams, 76
kuhina nui, x, xi, xii, 20, 23, 25, 42, 46, 48, 49, 50, 124, 125
Kūkāʻilimoku, xii, xiii, 14, 16, 27, 122
kuleana, x, 27
Kumulipo, 64
kūpuna, 110

L

Ladd & Company, 25
Lāhaināluna School, xii, xiii
    Seminary, 24
land, viii, ix, x, xiii, 3, 5, 19, 21, 25, 26, 27, 31, 51, 55, 57, 85, 101, 102, 109, 110, 111, 112, 125
lava, 51, 103
Law of the Splintered Paddle, 15, 123
Lee, William L., 25
lei niho palaoa, x, 9, 10
Leiopapa, Albert Edward Kauikeaouli, 30
Leleiōhoku, William Pitt, xiii, 49, 50, 51, 57, 58, 62, 68, 85, 89, 124
leprosy, 30
Liberal Party, 86
Liholiho, Alexander, vii, xiii, 17, 19, 20, 21, 23, 27, 29, 30, 31, 32, 33, 46, 49, 50, 52, 123, 125
Likelike, Miriam, xiii, 55, 68, 101, 103
    Princess, vi, 101, 103, 104, 128

Liliha, 21, 47, 48
Liliʻuokalani, Lydia, vi, vii, xi, xiii, 54, 55, 62, 64, 80, 81, 82, 85, 86, 87, 88, 89, 90, 92, 93, 94, 95, 96, 97, 98, 101, 102, 103, 104,, 105, 106, 109, 110, 111, 114, 116, 119
Lono, x, xiii, 2, 3
Lunalilo Home, 109, 126
Lunalilo, William Charles, vi, vii, xiii, 41, 42, 43, 52, 57, 62, 70, 76, 83, 109, 125, 126
L'Uranie, 20, 123

M

māhele, x, 26, 27
mahiole, x, 8, 10
makaʻāinana, x, 3
makahiki, x, xiii, 2, 3, 20, 82
Malietoa, Chief, 71
Malo, David, xiii, 5, 24
mana, viii, x, 2, 3, 4, 9, 17, 19, 24, 29, 41, 45, 47, 48, 51, 55, 54, 86, 116
Manuia Lanai, 64
Marignoli, 116
mele, x, 6, 86, 97
misprision of treason, 94, 128
missionary, xi, 9, 11, 24, 25, 29, 31, 51, 55, 57, 64, 65, 66, 80, 85, 86
Missionary Party, 66
missionary schools, 24
Moanalua, 79, 109
   Gardens, 79
moʻo aliʻi, x
motto, viii, 60, 125
music, 62, 85, 93
Mutsuhito, Emperor, 62

N

Naeʻole, 13
Nāhiʻenaʻena, 48, 49
Nāmāhana, 45
Neilson, Henry, 31, 33
nīʻaupiʻo x, 48
Nuʻuanu Pali, 16

O

Order of Kamehameha, 11
ʻōʻō, 7, 9
Osbourne, Lloyd, 65

P

Pacific, 4, 63, 71, 114

Pacific Commercial Advertiser, 11, 31, 71
Pākī, Abner, 85, 86
Parker, Eva, 104
   Sam, 50, 116
Patriotic League, 86
Pauahi, Bernice, vi, xii, xiii, 41, 50, 51, 54, 55, 68, 78, 80, 81, 82, 85, 109, 111, 112, 125, 127
Paulet, George, 27, 125
peacocks, 105
Pearl Harbor, 41, 85, 126
Pele, 51, 53, 103, 124
plantation, 11, 25, 30, 62, 88, 91
plebiscite, 41
Poor, Henry, 64
population, ix, 2, 21, 26, 27, 30, 37, 62, 68, 85, 110
Pride of Hawaiʻi, 21
priest, ix, 19, 25, 46, 47, 48, 123
Prince Lot Hula Festival, 79
Prince of Hawaiʻi, xii, 30, 31, 33, 52, 53, 77, 125
Princeville, 30
pūloʻuloʻu, x, 10, 121
Puʻukoholā, xii, 14, 121

Q

Queen Emma, vi, xiii, 30, 31, 33, 53, 57, 58, 68, 77, 83, 101, 109, 110, 125, 127
   Foundation, 110
   Summer Palace, 77
Queen Kamāmalu, 21, 23, 124
Queen's Hospital, 30, 110, 125
Queen's Medical Center, 110
Queen's Prayer, 93

R

reciprocity, 30, 41, 43, 62, 86, 88
regalia, 7, 9, 10, 11, 66
regent, x, 21, 46, 62, 89, 123, 126
Republic of Hawaiʻi, xi, 94, 96, 104, 128
revolution, 86, 88, 92, 93, 94, 114, 116
Robertson, James, 59
Rooke, Emma Naea, xiii, 29, 32, 51, 52, 125
Royal Boat House, 65
   Hawaiian Hotel, 79, 83
   Household Troops, 43, 70
   Mausoleum, vi, 69, 114, 120
   Order of Kamehameha, 120
   ring, 10
   seal, 26

S

Salazar, Owana Kaʻohelelani, 116, 117

Samuel M. Damon Estate, 79
scepter, 10
school, 24, 31, 51, 70, 78, 80, 101, 102, 106, 111, 112
Seaside Hotel, 83
smallpox, 21, 26
Spreckels, Claus, 66
Staley, Thomas, 31
statehood, 114
Stevens, John L., 88, 92, 94, 127
Stevenson, Robert Louis, 64, 65, 67, 83, 101, 102
sugar (sugarcane), 3, 30, 41, 62, 66, 88, 116, 124, 126

T

territory, 102, 104, 114, 128
Thaddeus, 21, 123
The Pacific Commercial Advertiser, 96
Thurston, Lorrin, 86, 102, 118
Tikhanov, Mikhail, 7, 8
Treaty of Annexation, 127
    of Reciprocity, 127

U

Uluniu, 82

United States, xiii, 29, 30, 41, 53, 54, 62, 63, 66, 71, 85, 88, 92, 93, 94, 103, 104, 111, 114, 116, 112, 124, 125, 126, 127, 128

V

volcano, 53, 124

W

Waikīkī, 17, 53, 79, 82, 101, 105, 106, 107, 111, 123, 128
Washington Place, 81, 88, 89, 93, 94, 95, 96, 97, 125, 126, 128
whalers, 21, 24
whaling, 125
Wilcox, Robert, xiii, 70, 86, 93, 116, 127, 128
Wodehouse, James, 53
writing, 14, 24
Wyllie, 25, 29, 30, 33

Y

Young, John, 14, 15, 29, 51, 77
Young, John, II, 26

Hawaiian Ali'i Genealogy Chart

Legend:
- ■ man
- ● woman
- ▬▬ marriage
- * This individual repeats in more than one place

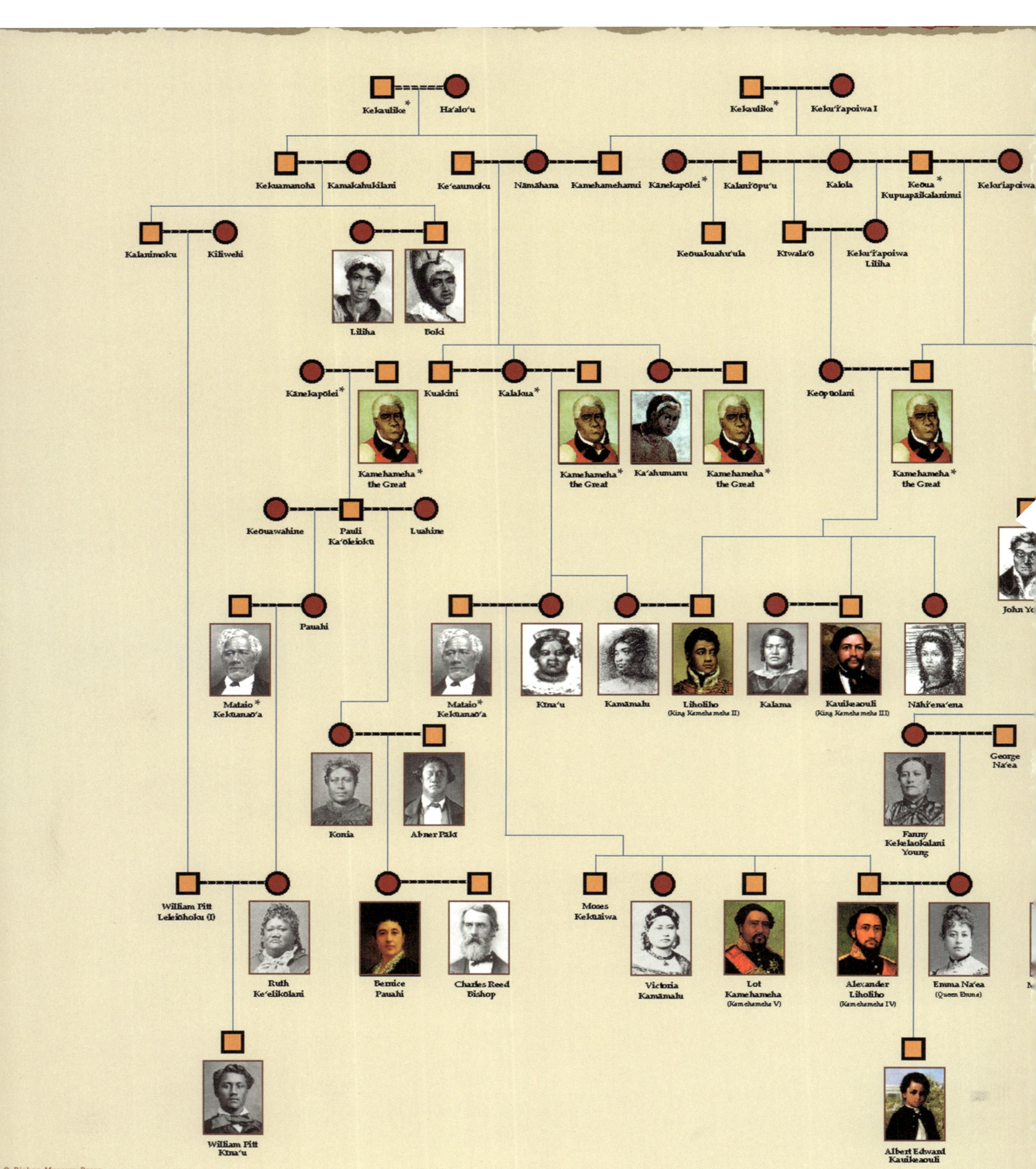

Generation 1
- Kekaulike* ⚭ Ha'alo'u
- Kekaulike* ⚭ Keku'iapoiwa I

Generation 2
- Kekuamanoha ⚭ Kamakahukilani
- Ke'eaumoku ⚭ Namahana
- Kamehamehanui
- Kanekapōlei* ⚭ Kalani'ōpu'u ⚭ Kalola
- Keoua Kupuapaikalaninui* ⚭ Keku'iapoiwa

Generation 3
- Kalanimoku ⚭ Kiliwehi
- Liliha ⚭ Boki
- Keouakuahu'ula
- Kiwala'ō ⚭ Keku'iapoiwa Liliha

Generation 4
- Kanekapōlei* ⚭ Kuakini
- Kalakua* ⚭ Kamehameha the Great
- Kamehameha the Great ⚭ Ka'ahumanu
- Kamehameha the Great
- Keōpūolani ⚭ Kamehameha the Great

Generation 5
- Keouawahine ⚭ Pauli Ka'ōleiokū ⚭ Luahine
- John Young

Generation 6
- Pauahi ⚭ Mataio* Kekūanao'a
- Mataio* Kekūanao'a ⚭ Kīna'u
- Kamāmalu
- Liholiho (King Kamehameha II)
- Kalama ⚭ Kauikeaouli (King Kamehameha III)
- Nāhi'ena'ena ⚭ George Na'ea

Generation 7
- Konia ⚭ Abner Pākī
- Fanny Kekelaokalani Young

Generation 8
- William Pitt Leleiōhoku (I) ⚭ Ruth Ke'elikōlani
- Bernice Pauahi ⚭ Charles Reed Bishop
- Moses Kekūaiwa
- Victoria Kamāmalu
- Lot Kamehameha (Kamehameha V)
- Alexander Liholiho (Kamehameha IV) ⚭ Emma Na'ea (Queen Emma)

Generation 9
- William Pitt Kīna'u
- Albert Edward Kauikeaouli

© Bishop Museum Press
Based on a chart by Anne Harding Spoehr.

This chart shows the best-known Hawaiian ali'i, but it is not intended to be complete. Pictures are not available for many of the individuals listed here.